Shirley Whitehead's Madeira Walks

(2nd edition)

with

Shirley Whitehead

DISCOVERY WALKING GUIDES LTD

Shirley Whitehead's Madeira Walks
First Edition published July 2006
Second Edition published September 2011

Published by
Discovery Walking Guides Ltd
10 Tennyson Close, Northampton NN5 7HJ,
England

Maps
Maps sections are taken from **Madeira Tour & Trail Super-Durable Map** published by **Discovery Walking Guides Ltd**.

Photographs
The photographs in this book were taken by the author and co-walkers.

Front Cover Photographs

Levada do Norte (Walk 37)

Calhau from the cliff-top path (Walk 15)

Levada Nova (Walk 5)

On Pico Grande (Walk 2)

ISBN 9781904946557

The author and publishers have tried to ensure that the information and maps in this publication are as accurate as possible. However, we accept no responsibility for any loss, injury or inconvenience sustained by anyone using this book.

Shirley Whitehead's Madeira Walks

CONTENTS

WALKS IN THE CENTRAL EAST REGION

WALKS IN THE SOUTH-EAST & NORTH-EAST REGIONS

THE AUTHOR

Shirley Whitehead settled in Madeira in 2002 and lives in Jardim do Mar on the south west coast. Born in Lancashire, England, she lived for many years in West Yorkshire where she developed a keen interest in the natural and built environment and enjoyed walking in the Yorkshire Dales as well the Peak and Lake Districts.

Since moving to Madeira she has spent much of her time discovering the island's diverse landscape and its natural and cultural history, walking the *levadas*, forest trails, moorland and mountain tracks and coastal routes as well as visiting many of the towns, village and hamlet across the island.

Shirley is a regular contributor to 'The Brit' newspaper, writing articles on walking and heritage.

This publication is a complete re-write of her first walking guide, which together with her second book **Walk! Madeira** (ISBN 9781904946694) which was researched and written jointly with her husband, is published by Discovery Walking Guides Ltd.

ACKNOWLEDGEMENT

My sincere thanks to my husband Mike for his enthusiasm for the project, his companionship when walking the routes, his patience proof reading and for the tremendous amount of technical support in producing this publication, which I could not have achieved without him.

PREFACE

Until quite recently, writing walking guides on Madeira was a relatively easy exercise. In many respects, notwithstanding the extensive development of the island's infrastructure, time stands still here and temperate weather conditions prevail. But, not so in 2010 when the island suffered some of the worst conditions in recent times. The February floods and landslides devastated many areas, damaging 90% of the *levadas* to a greater or lesser extent. Then during August a second disaster struck, when fire ravaged huge sections of the central massif closing almost all the high altitude walking routes and destroying 95% of the **Funchal Ecological Park**.

But nature is a powerful healer and now, twelve months on, and after extensive commitment and investment by the regional government, I can report that almost all the walking routes across the island have been reopened and Madeira is again a green, beautiful and a safe destination for walkers.

This book, first published in 2006, has now been re-researched and completely rewritten to take account of the problems suffered in 2010; all routes that had been subjected to substantial damage have been re-walked and checked for safety and accuracy.

This updated edition of **Shirley Whitehead's Madeira Walks** serves as a companion to **Walk! Madeira** - jointly researched and written by Shirley and Mike Whitehead - updated in late 2010 and also published by Discovery Walking Guides Ltd. Together these two publications are now the most thorough and up to date guides for the Garden Island.

The new edition includes over forty alternative trails, some 'off the beaten track ' routes whilst others are variations of the island's 'Recommended Trails for Hikers', or intersect with them. At the date of publication, 24 of the official routes had been opened, all of which are summarized within the relevant walks text in this publication and are also cross-referenced to the Walk! Madeira guide.

Information on the island's 'Recommended Trails for Hikers' and the programme of 'Access for All'including routes suitable for the blind and disabled, is given in the walking section.

All routes included have been surveyed and mapped using GPS satellite navigation and the author has walked all the trails between 2009 and 2011, thus ensuring accuracy and up to date information. Clear descriptions guide the walker both to the starting point of the walks and throughout the routes, with gradings, distances, timings and altitudes all symbolized. Information on flora and fauna is also included while references to places of interest give readers a sense of the culture and history around these trails. Map sections were developed from the **Madeira Tour & Trail Map**, by far the most up to date and best-selling map on the island.

INTRODUCTION

The north coast

Madeira is a wonderful destination for walkers offering a truly breathtaking diversity of landscape; its lushly vegetated slopes, towering volcanic peaks, dramatic gorges and soaring cliffs, take visitors by surprise. Add to this the *levada* network, the primeval forests, the subtropical flora and the superb landscaped gardens - little wonder then that the island is often referred to as, "The floating garden of the Atlantic".

TOPOGRAPHY

The archipelago is situated in the eastern Atlantic around 950 kilometres south of mainland Portugal and 600 kilometres west of Morocco. It consists of the principal island of Madeira, **Porto Santo**, the **Desertas** and the **Selvagens**; the latter two being uninhabited nature reserves protected by the **Parque Natural da Madeira**. Together with the Azores, Canaries and the Cape Verde Islands, these archipelagos form a bio-geographic region referred to as Macaronesia.

With a population of c267,000, Madeira's economy consists of small to medium size industry, tourism and some agriculture, mostly wine. The main island is around 57 kilometres long and 23 kilometres wide; the central massif includes the peaks of **Pico Ruivo** (1862m), **Pico do Areeiro** (1818m) and **Pico das Torres** (1852m). The north coast boasts steep, tall sea cliffs; the most extreme however is **Cabo Girão** on the south coast, being the highest in Europe and second highest in the world. The neighbouring island of **Porto Santo** is renowned for its magnificent sandy beach, seven kilometres long.

CLIMATE

Madeira enjoys a temperate year-round climate with average daytime temperatures around the coast of 18°C-24°C. Generally speaking, the north is wetter and cloudier than the south, while along the island's mountainous spine, the weather is subject to rapid change and can be windy, wet and cloudy - and occasionally, snowy. There's a useful website (www.netmadeira.com) giving hourly updates via web cam photographs, on weather conditions across the island.

THE LEVADAS

Although irrigation channels are not unique to Madeira, the island undoubtedly boasts some of the world's finest examples. There are over 200 *levadas*, covering 1500 kilometres, with new channels still being constructed. Historically built for irrigation to bring water from the wetter north to the arid southern areas, the *levadas* later became important for hydropower. Most slope gently - almost imperceptibly in some cases - as they follow the natural contours of the terrain, providing ideal walking where accompanying paths

A carved tunnel carries a *levada*

allow. Where the shape of the land gets in the way, tunnels have been pushed through to take the channels. From the walker's point of view, the *levadas* not only provide memorable and beautiful walking experiences, they open up otherwise impenetrable regions of the island's interior. *Levadeiros* (Levada Workers) are charged with keeping the channels and pathways in good condition and the *levada* keepers' cottages, usually surrounded by well-planted gardens, can be found along many of the routes.

Protea species from South Africa

FLORA AND FAUNA

The Laurisilva

The island's name means 'wood', so named by early settlers who found it almost totally covered by great forests of mainly Lauraceae species, but over the centuries the trees were used for timber and the lower woodlands were burnt to release land for farming and pastures.

Newer forests of pine, acacia (Mimosaceae), eucalyptus and oak now occupy much of the *laurisilva's* former territory. Nevertheless, the natural forest of Madeira is the largest area of *laurisilva* in the world. It covers 150 sq. km (58 square miles) representing just over 20% of the island's surface. Many of the plants evolved millions of years ago and the *laurisilva* survives now only in Central Macaronesia.

Due to their importance these subtropical humid forests were classified a World Nature Heritage Site in 1999 by UNESCO.

Echium Candicans, Paúl da Serra

Plants and Trees

Given its climate and the fertile volcanic soil, Madeira is a botanical paradise renowned for luxurious sub-tropical vegetation where species from all over the world thrive in gardens and avenues. There are over 1300 species of indigenous and naturalized plants of which around 150 are endemic. Vineyards and banana plantations dominate the lower coastal areas and along the agricultural terraces you'll find exotic fruit trees of papaya, fig, mango, avocado, orange and lemon. The main vegetable crops include sweet potato, beans, tomatoes and various types of brassicas.

Birds

There are a number of Important Bird Areas (IBA's) within the archipelago with around 250 bird species and subspecies recorded, although only around 42 breed regularly. The only true endemics are the long-toed pigeon (Columba trocaz), which inhabits the *laurisilva*, and the Zino's petrel (Pterodroma Madeira), breeding on the cliff tops and mountains. There are however a number of endemic sub-species, as well as Macaronesian endemics. SPEA-Madeira is the Portuguese Society for the Protection of Birds and is a partner of Birdlife International. Information on publications for bird watching areas is given in Appendix D.

Monarch butterfly

Animals

No mammals other than bats occur naturally. The only endemic reptile species is the Madeiran Wall Lizard (Teira dugesii). Insects include grasshoppers, crickets and migratory locusts, plus many butterflies, the beautiful Monarch being the largest species on the island.

Aquatic mammals include a number of species of whales and dolphins, which can sometimes be observed from the coastal areas, and the endangered Mediterranean Monk Seal, now thriving around the **Desertas** islands and occasionally seen off the coastline of Madeira; turtles are also quite commonly seen in the coastal waters.

WALKING

Following the adverse weather conditions in 2010, most walking routes have now been reopened and are safe to walk. However, due to the islands isolation in the Atlantic and its natural mountainous terrain, isolated problems do occur from time to time, albeit on a much small scale. Landslips and *levada* maintenance occasionally have the effect of closing routes; nevertheless Madeira is still a beautiful and safe destination for walkers. We suggest that if in doubt before setting out on any trail, visitors should check with their hotel reception or the Tourist offices which receive regular bulletins from the authorities and can advise on the current status of most routes.

Trails and Paths

The selection of walks included in this publication provide something for everyone, regardless of individual ability and fitness and range from gentle strolls to challenging routes. Terrain on the routes varies widely. Some *levada* walks, although long, are on flat, easy paths with negligible ascents and descents; others require far more concentration on narrow paths, perhaps with sheer drops or on slippery, poor surfaces.

The official "Recommended Trails for Hikers"
Over the past decade, the island's infrastructure and facilities have undergone extensive development; not least has been the substantial investment to improve walking trails helping make Madeira one of Europe's top hiking destinations.

Twenty five routes across the island, have been designated 'Recommended Trails for Hikers' by the Regional Government, all being upgraded, signed and made safer for the public.

This programme of 'Access for All' continues to increase the scope and variety of walking routes throughout the island, with a number now created specifically for disabled people, using the unique 'Joelette' cycles. One route for blind people and three additional routes for cyclists have also been created. See Appendix C for details.

Summaries of the routes opened prior to spring 2011 are referred to in the walks text and are referenced with PR numbers, an abbreviation of the Portuguese *pequeno rota* (small routes). These trails were surveyed with GPS Satellite navigation between 2008-2010; see **Walk! Madeira** for full walking notes. A list of official PR recommended Trails for Hikers is given in Appendix C.

APR route information panel

Preparation
Be prepared - read through the walk description before you set out, and take note of the information bar for each route.

Exertion ratings range from 1 (easy) to 5 (strenuous); these are inevitably subjective and will depend on, for example, age and fitness. The time taken for each route is my recorded time and does not include stops for taking photos or refreshments. Timings and distances on linear routes refer as follows:

1. One way, where there are options for private or public transport at the end of the walk or,
2. Return times for those routes requiring retracing our steps back to the starting point.

Distance is shown in kilometres, and ascents and descents in metres. Vertigo risk ranges from 0 (no risk) to 3 (high vertigo risk). Note that the vertigo risk often applies to only a short section of the route, although if you're a sufferer, it can feel like the longest few metres you've ever walked. (See symbols ratings guide).

Safety - Do take safety seriously:-
Please note that there is no organised mountain rescue service in Madeira; incidents are dealt with by a combination of Ambulance, Fire and Police services.

The Regional Government accepts no responsibility for personal injury or damage of property and therefore we are individually responsible for our own safety. We suggest the following checklist:-

- Don't take risks. If you find a route made impassable by, for example, a landslide, then turn back. Attempting to find your own way through can be highly dangerous, especially on newly fallen slides. Look for the signs; if the landslip has been levelled or boarded by the *levadeiros,* then it is usually safe to cross.

- Take note of local weather forecasts (remember that weather changes happen swiftly on mountainous islands, especially at altitude). Turn back if bad weather sets in.

- Start out early and plan to finish well before dusk. Let someone know (at your hotel, for example) where you plan to walk and what time you expect to be back, and if possible walk with a companion.

- Go properly equipped with an up to date map and guide book and a torch for all routes with tunnels. GPS is desirable but not essential; a compass at least is recommended.

- Clothing, including footwear, should be up to the job and should include a light raincoat and fleece when going into the mountains.

- Take lots of water with you and food on longer walks

- If possible take a mobile phone and emergency contact numbers although you should bear in mind that mobile phones may not always work in remote parts of the island.

GETTING AROUND

Hire cars and taxis are the most convenient way of getting around; since the completion of the Rápida (VR1) and other major (VE) highways, accessibility to all areas of the island is relatively quick and easy. Hire cars are available at the airport and from hotels and agencies in **Funchal** and around the island. Taxis are another option at reasonable cost. Drivers will take you to the start of each walk and, if required, will collect you at the end. Taxis can be hired for half or full days; drivers carry standard price lists for journeys outside **Funchal**. See Appendix A for taxi phone numbers.

Bus journeys can be an adventure; many of the walks in this book can be accessed by public transport (see each walk introduction). Special tickets make this good value. We recommend the latest edition of **Madeira Bus & Touring Map** (Published by Discovery Walking Guides Ltd), invaluable for bus users and car drivers alike. Timetables can be purchased from bus and newspaper kiosks in **Funchal**. (See also Appendix D for Bus Information, including website addresses for the main operators on the island).

The following are some of my favourites, worthy of particular mention.

GARDENS

Monte Palace Tropical Gardens

Acquired by the Barardo Foundation in 1987 these beautiful gardens occupy 70,000 m^2. Planted with exotic flora from around the world and with magnificent water features including waterfalls and lagoons, the entire gardens are enhanced with wonderful works of art. There are two museums; one houses a mineral and gem collection while the second displays a huge collection of Zimbabwe contemporary sculpture.

Palheiro Gardens and Quinta do Ferreiro

Bought by the Blandy wine family in the late 1800s, the **Palheiro Gardens** are famous for their diversity of plants, magnificent trees and their beautiful setting in the hills to the east of **Funchal**.

Magnolia, Palheiro Gardens

Quinta do Arco Rose Garden, Arco de Sã Jorge

The Rose Garden has recently received international recognition from the World Federation of Rose Societies; 17,000 roses and 1,450 species are on display; there's also a lovely restaurant at **Quinta do Arco**.

Jardim Botânico da Madeira

opened in 1960, this 80 acre garden is home to more than 2,500 plant species, 300 exotic birds and 200 species of indigenous plants. The gardens can be accessed by the *teleférico*, the one from **Babosas Square** descending directly into the *parque*.

NATURE RESERVES

Núcleo de Dragoeiros das Neves

A nature conservation centre close to **São Gonçalo** east of **Funchal**, this reserve houses a small museum in a former farmhouse.

Dracaena draco

The gardens are dedicated to indigenous plant species of the coastal areas of Madeira including a magnificent group of centuries-old dragon trees (Dracaena draco) a Macaronesian endemic once in abundance on the island but now almost extinct. Only two survive naturally, near **Ribeira Brava**.

Posto Florestal - Ribeiro Frio

This reserve displays a collection of endemic plants specific to the *laurisilva* and in summer, you'll find (amongst many others) the rare yellow foxglove (Isoplexis sceptrum), Musschia wollastonii and carrot trees. It's also the site of a trout farm and fish hatchery, providing brown trout to replenish Madeira's watercourses.

NATURAL HISTORY MUSEUMS

Rota da Cal (The Lime Route)

A new museum in **Lamaceiros** village, **São Vicente** and a unique site of geological and botanical importance, **Rota da Cal** is situated in a sea limestone outbreak with fossils over 5 million years old and is also an area of *laurisilva*, attracting endemic bird species and subspecies and numerous species of endemic flora.

Aquário da Madeira, Porto Moniz

A small aquarium opened in 2005 in the wonderful old **São João** fort next to the harbour in **Porto Moniz**; its interior is superb, inspired by the surrounding marine environment.

Aquário da Madeira Porto Moniz

Volcano Centre and Caves São Vicente

This cultural and learning centre focusing on Madeira's volcanic origins offers a number of daily guided tours through the caves (**Grutas de São Vicente**) and lava tubes, plus exhibitions and exciting film of the journey of the island.

For opening times and contact details for the Gardens, Nature Reserve and Natural History Museums, please refer to Appendix B.

OTHER THINGS TO DO

A Trip to the Desertas Islands

The Gavião Luxury Yacht sails to the uninhabited nature reserve of the **Desertas**, habitat of the endangered monk seal and rare wildlife bird sanctuary. Moor in a sheltered cove of the **Deserta Grande**, then go ashore to visit the guard's accommodation and the information centre. The round trip from **Funchal** marina takes around 7-8 hours and includes lunch and refreshments.

Sail on the Santa Maria (Replica of Columbus's vessel)

Daily sails leave **Funchal** harbour usually heading for **Cabo Girão**. This wonderful vessel offers the chance to see whales and dolphins, coastal sightseeing and swimming in marvellous turquoise waters below the highest cliff.

Dolphin & Whale watching from Calheta

Take a sail on the Ilhéu, a 1946 Gaffing Ketch making 3hr daytime trips and sunset trips from the **Calheta** marina or from **Madelena do Mar**.

Santa Maria below Cabo Girão

Discover Funchal

Jacarandas in bloom, Funchal

Take a stroll from the famous **Reid's Palace Hotel** along jacaranda-lined avenues. En-route you'll pass beside the President's residency, **Quinta Vigia** and the magnificent **Santa Catarina Park** on the right, across from which is **Dona Amélia Garden** and lower down, the exotic **Municipal Park** in the city centre.

Palacio e Fortaleza de São Lourenço

This short walk takes you past the wonderful **Palácio e Fortaleza de São Lourenço** and the famous **Golden Gate Café** before arriving at **Sé Catedral** (built 1485-1514), one of Madeira's oldest buildings.

Visit Funchal's Zona Velha (Old Town)

Pavement cafés in Zona Velha

Visit the famous and colourful produce market, then wander along **Rua D. Carlos** with its pretty pavement restaurants and lovely chapel, before arriving at **São Trigo Fortress** housing a modern art gallery and a wonderful restaurant.

Coastal Resorts

Visit the towns of **Santa Cruz**, **Machico** and **Porto da Cruz** or take a drive along the stunning north coast to **Porto Moniz**. A visit to many of these towns can be linked to the walks starting or ending close to these areas.

São Trigo Fortress

Santa Cruz beach

The Teleférico to Rocha do Navio Nature Reserve

Take a cable car ride on the Teleférico

There are six operating around the island serving the following areas: -

- **Funchal**, sea front to **Monte**
- **Babosas** to the **Botanical Gardens**

Cristo Rei

- **Garajau** to the beachside complex - (besides the impressive statue of Christ, a replica of the Rio statue)
- **Achadas da Cruz** to the *fajá* and vineyards at beach level
- **Rancho**, **Cãmara de Lobos**, to the agricultural areas at sea level
- **Rocha do Navio, Santana** to the vineyards and islets along the coast

Fajã dos Padres

A lift rather than cable car takes you down to **Fája dos Padros** at **Cabo Girão**, for sun, sea, food and wine and a fantastic place to wander around along cobbled pathways to the cottages, vineyards and orchards.

Visit Fortim do Faial

Cannons at the lookout, Faial

This small mock fort complete with 10 cannons (built between 18th-19thC) is really a lookout point or monument built by the Catanho de Maneses family commanding wonderful views along the north coast over **Faial**, **Porto da Cruz** and **Eagle Rock**.

Information and contact details for other activities including sailing, whale and dolphin watching, bird watching and canyoning are given in Appendix B.

MAP PROVENANCE

Simplified and adapted map data provided by **Discovery Walking Guides Ltd**. (copyright David Brawn) has been used to prepare this locator map.

The latest editions of **Madeira Tour & Trail Map** and **Madeira Bus & Touring Map** are available from:

www.walking.demon.co.uk
www.dwgwalking.co.uk

Digital mapping for a variety of destinations including Madeira is available from:

www.instant-books.org
Mapyx QUO www.mapyx.com
Memory-Map www.memory-map.co.uk

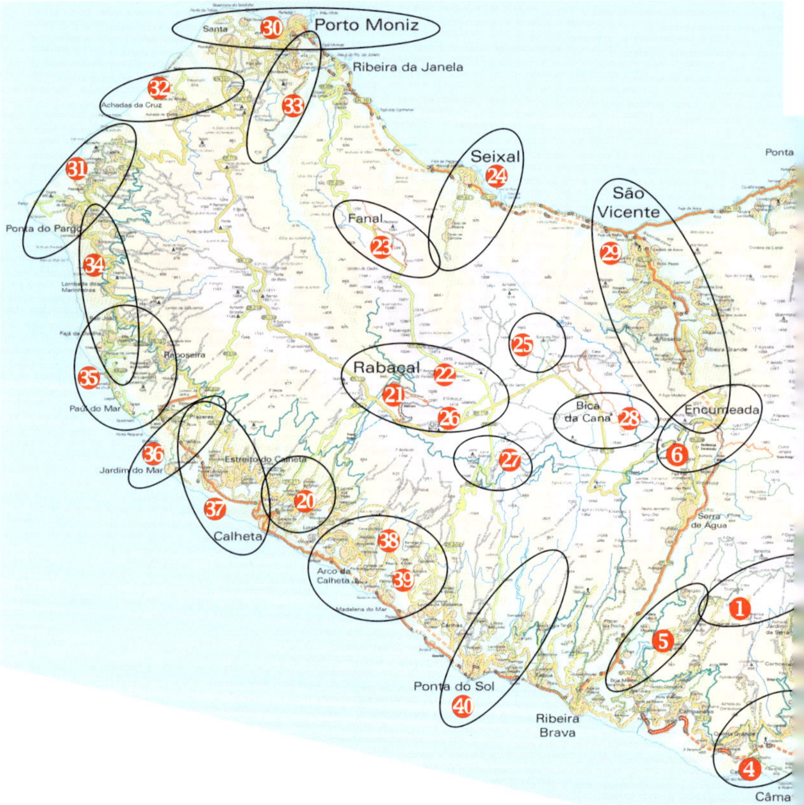

Please Note:

This locator map is intended to give a general indication of each walk area.

In order to avoid confusion, where two or more walks share a similar area, only one elipse common to that group has been drawn.

WALK LOCATOR MAP

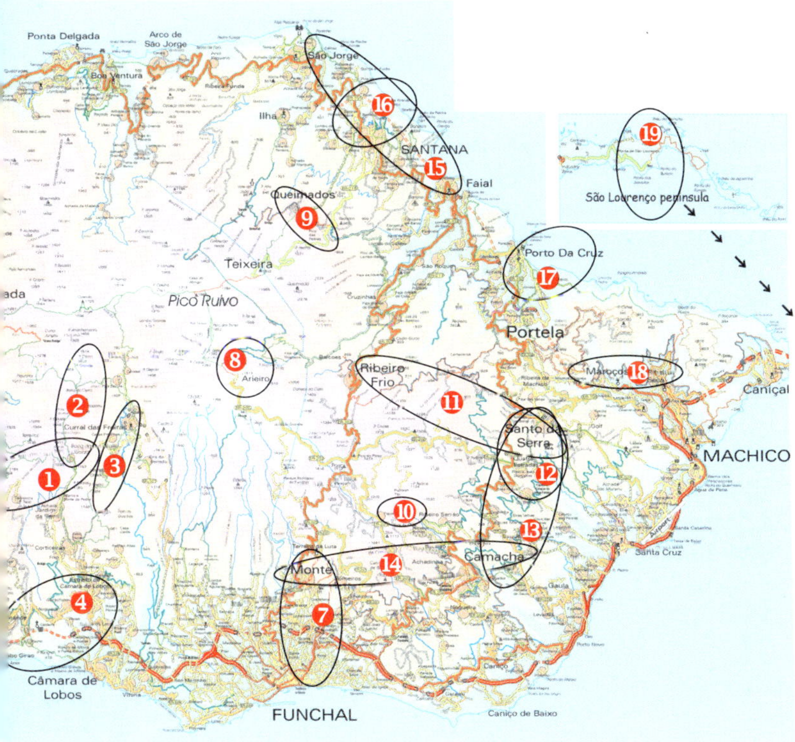

MAP NOTES AND LEGEND

The map sections in this book have been adapted from **Madeira Tour & Trail Map** published by **Discovery Walking Guides Ltd. Madeira Tour & Trail Map**, and **Madeira Bus & Touring Map**, are available from:

Discovery Walking Guides Ltd.
21 Upper Priory Street
Northampton NN1 2PT

- or online at www.walking.demon.co.uk and www.dwgwalking.co.uk

Digital mapping for destinations including Madeira can be found at:
www.instant-books.org
Mapyx QUO www.mapyx.com
Memory-Map www.memory-map.co.uk

Madeira Tour & Trail Legend-Legende

ALTITUDE, HÖHE, ALTITUD, ALTITUDE

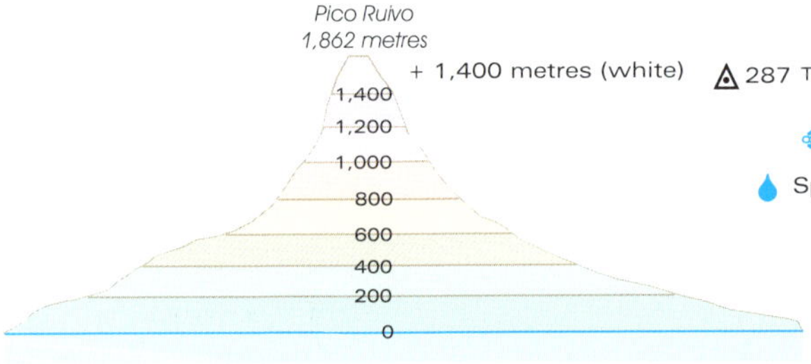

• 186 Height
287 Trig Point Height
Miradouro viewpoint
Spring, Fonte
Sea (0 metres)

ROADS, STRAßE, CARRETERA, ROUTE

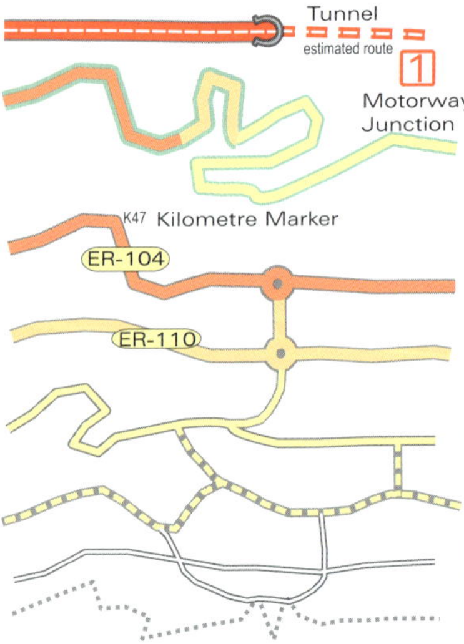

Via Rapida, Motorway, Autobahn, Autopista.

Scenic Driving Routes
Landschaftlich schöne Strecke
Recorrido pintoresco
Parcours pittoresque

Main road, Haupstraße, Carretera principal,Route à grande circulation

Secondary road, Regionalstraße, Carretera, Route

Minor road, Lokalstraße, Carretera, Route secondaire

Narrow road, Fahrweg, Camino Rural, Chemin carrosable

Dirt road, Fahrweg, Camino, Chemin carrosable

Path, Fußweg, Sendero, Sentier

Gardens

Teleférico Cable Car

Urban area

Tower, Torre · Lighthouse, Faro · Pylon · Picnic area

Chapel, Capela · Church, Igreja · P Parking · Bar/Rest

Hotel · Petrol · Sports Ground, Campo Desportivo

Camping · Cemetery, Cemitério · Wind Turbine, Eólica

Information · Vertiginous section of route

Forest House, Posto Florestal · *Rib* Ribeira, River · *Lev* Levada, Canal

Walking Routes, Wanderweg, Sendero, Chemin

Walk! Madeira & Shirley Whitehead's Madeira Walks

Walking Routes (Red) with route numbers

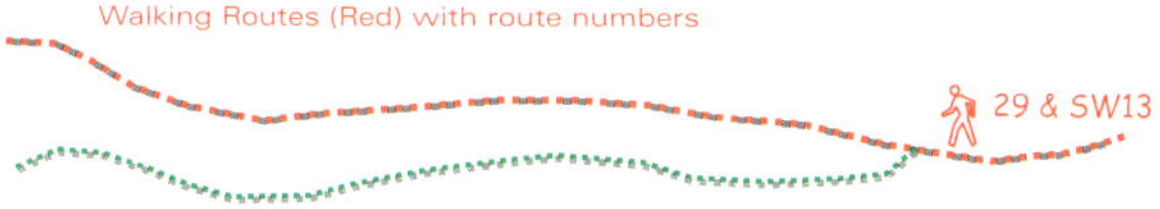

Alternative walking routes and other published walking routes (Green)

SYMBOLS RATING GUIDE

3 our rating for effort/exertion:-
1 very easy **2** easy
3 average **4** energetic
5 strenuous

2½ H approximate **time** to complete a walk (compare your times against ours early in a walk) - does not include stopping time

8.5km approximate walking **distance** in kilometres

250m 850m approximate **ascents/descents** in metres (N=negligible)

circular route

linear route

figure of eight route

2 risk of **vertigo** - from 1-some risk to 3-high risk

3 **refreshments** (may be at start or end of a route only)

Walk descriptions include:

- timing in minutes, shown as (40M)
- compass directions, shown as (NW)
- heights in metres, shown as (1355m)
- GPS waypoints, shown as (Wp.3)

Notes on the text

Place names are shown in **bold text**, except where we refer to a written sign, when they are enclosed in single quotation marks. Local or unusual words are shown in *italics*, and are explained in the accompanying text.

GPS' 'pinpoint navigational accuracy' can be a great benefit for walkers, especially when tackling landscapes you have not seen before. Using a GPS with our waypoints you will be reassured that you are both in the right place and going the right way - very reassuring for first time visitors (and regular visitors) to Madeira. Each waypoint symbol shown on the map for each walk is numbered, so that it can be directly identified against the walk description and waypoint list.

To Input the Waypoints

GPS waypoint co-ordinates are quoted for the WGS84 datum, in degrees and minutes of Latitude and Longitude. To input the waypoints into your GPS we suggest that you:-

- switch on your GPS and select 'simulator' mode or 'operate with GPS off' depending upon which GPS model you are using.
- check that your GPS is set to the WGS84 datum (its default datum) and the 'location format' 'hddd° .mm.mmm'.
- input the GPS Waypoints into a 'Route' file (note this is the Route in your GPS, a collection of Waypoints, and should not be confused with a walking route description) with the same number as the walking route number; then when you call up the 'Route' on Madeira there will be no confusion as to which walking route it refers to.
- repeat the inputting of routes until you have covered all the routes you plan to walk, or until you have used up the memory capacity of your GPS; even the most basic of GPS units will store up to 20 GPS Routes of up to 50 waypoints for each GPS Route, and you can always re-programme your GPS while on Madeira.
- turn off your GPS.

When you turn the GPS back on it should return to its normal navigation mode. Note that GPS waypoints complement the detailed walking route descriptions and are not intended as an alternative to the detailed walking route description.

Personal Navigator Files (PNFs)

Edited versions of the original GPS research tracks and waypoints are available as downloadable files. In addition to Madeira, files are available for Tenerife, La Gomera, La Palma, Lanzarote, Mallorca, Menorca, Brittany, Calais and Boulogne, Andorra, Axarquia, Aracena and Alpujarras; plus GPS Utility Special Edition software and all of our Walk! UK series of guidebooks. See DWG websites for more information:

www.walking.demon.co.uk & www.dwgwalking.co.uk

1 BOCA DA CORRIDA - CHÃO DOS TERREIROS - FONTES

Boca da Corrida viewpoint and forestry house lie on a mountain ridge 1235m above sea level. The house is surrounded by woodland and there's a lovely shrine dedicated to **São Cristovão** sitting beside the car park. There's also a magnificent *miradouro* with views down the deep depression of **Nun's Valley** and across to the highest peaks.

It's the first of two routes starting at **Boca da Corrida**, both of which cross high altitude terrain and should only be undertaken in good weather. If cloud sets in you are advised to turn back immediately. Walking poles are recommended for both these routes as well as a hat, sun cream and lots of water.

This route climbs 200 metres to the summit of **Terreiros**, revealing some of the most dramatic and spectacular views on the island before leading us across a mountain trail to the village of **Fontes**. The area across **Chão dos Terreiros** to **Fontes** which suffered fire damage in 2010 is recovering remarkably well, the ground cover now completely green again; nevertheless, some aspects of the routes may vary from the descriptions given.

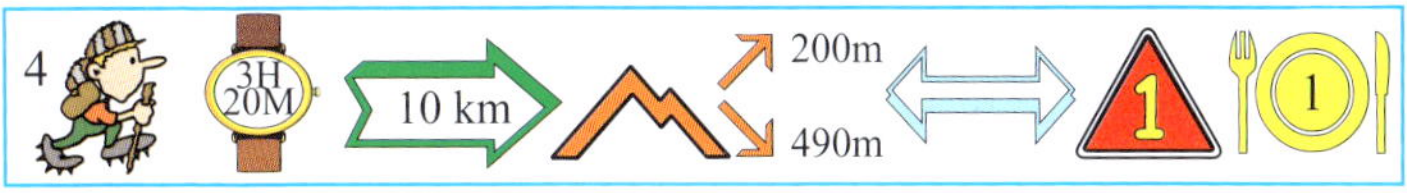

Access by car or taxi:
Take the ER229 to **Estreito de Cãmara de Lobos** church then follow the signs for 'Jardim da Serra'. From here continue up the access road to the **Boca da Corrida Forestry Post**, a total of 10.2 km from the VR1.

Access by bus:
Bus N°96 serves **Jardim da Serra** as far as **Bar Mario** below **Corrida**. It's then around 2 km with a 350 metre ascent to **Boca da Corrida**, so obviously taxis or private hire cars are the best options for reaching the starting point.

We leave **Corrida** car park (Wp.1 0M) on the cobbled track between the house and shrine, passing beside an information panel and steps on our right; this is **PR12**, the official walking route to **Pico Grande** and **Encumeada**.

Ignoring this, we go straight ahead, passing around the gateposts and chain link barrier signed 'Terreiros' and 'Aviceiros' to continue up the unmade vehicle track which bends left behind the forestry post. The track begins to ascend quite steeply as it winds and contours the hillside: there are superb views of **Funchal** to the south and the mountain range to the east.

Leaving Corrida

Shortly after the road levels out, we arrive at a junction with a track off to the right (Wp.2 35M); straight ahead goes to **Montado dos Aviceiros**, but here our route turns right, arriving five minutes later at a concrete building, formerly a sheep shelter.

The track continues to the front of the building, but at the first concrete post we leave the track on a right hand grassy path running parallel to the track (Wp.3 38M); red arrows painted on stones indicating the direction.

.. magnificent views (Wp.4) ..

The path heads up behind the shelter before climbing the hillside, after a few minutes reaching a fork in the path, where we continue straight ahead and arrive on a mountain ridge on the edge of a vast valley. Here we find one of the most magnificent views to be seen on Madeira; it's dramatic (Wp.4 55M).

Looking across to our left, **Chão dos Terreiros** is now clearly in view, its northern escarpment bare rock, the remainder covered in vegetation. Picking out a line of fencing running vertical from the ridge to the summit, we then head for this point.

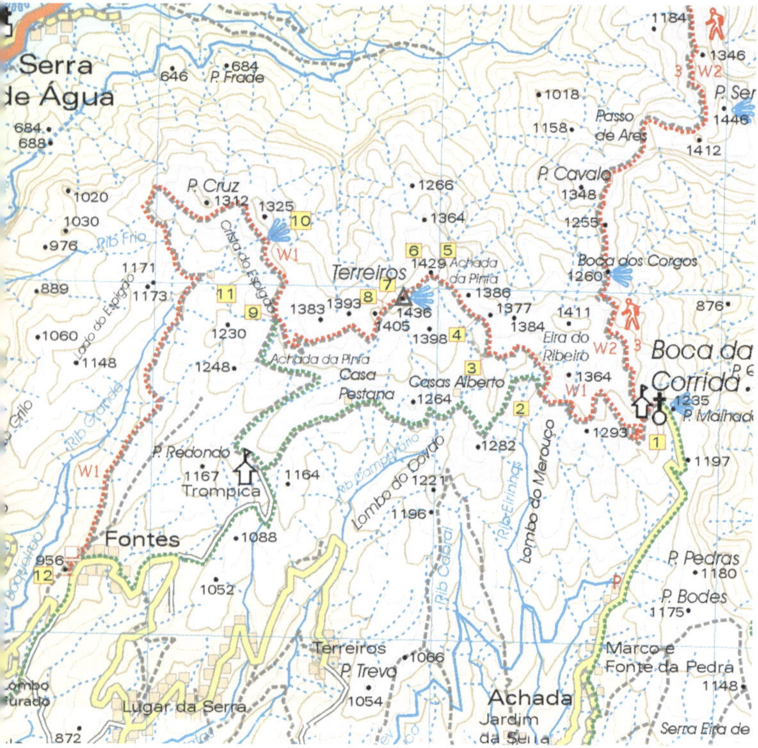

The path across the ridge is fairly rocky and a little vague in places, but soon we pick up the red way markings, which from hereon appear every few metres. The ridge is quite wide with no danger if we keep to the path and if visibility is good; however, care is needed along this section.

After fifteen minutes, on reaching the line of fencing and following it for a short distance, the path veers right and we find ourselves directly below the peak (Wp.5 75M). Here a vague narrow path ascends left to climb the escarpment; it's a relatively steep section and is very rocky underfoot, though the red marking will guide our way.

As the path heads back towards the fencing, it starts to zigzag up the final section and in a little over ten minutes from the start of the ascent, reaches a grassy plateau below the summit (Wp.6 90M).

The view from the ridge

It's worth spending a little time here to take in the panoramic views from the top of the northern escarpment, in clear weather **Paúl da Serra** and **Encumeada** are in view to the west and the central massif and **Nun's Valley** to the east; it's a wonderful viewpoint.

Veering left and dropping down the grassy path to reach the corner of the fencing, a gap in the stonewalling appears with more red markings; passing through the gap, our route turns immediately left to follow the line of fencing, a few minutes later reaching the trig point at 1435metres (Wp.7 100M).

Just beyond the trig point we pass over a stone style and head down the hillside bearing slightly left to reach a wide grassy area before picking up a vehicle track (Wp.8). Going left along the track, we drop down the hillside in a southerly direction soon arriving at a gate. Continuing along the track and passing through another gate, our trail arrives at the main **Trompica** track (Wp.9 125M) leading down the valley to the Forestry Post (1200m).

Our route turns right here to follow the track, soon reaching a viewpoint on our right (Wp.10 133M), then continuing on to the first pass where, throughout spring and summer, brightly coloured thistles, foxgloves and canary buttercups adorn the route. Cattle graze freely in this area and wonderful panoramic views open up all around us.

.. cattle graze freely ..

It's spectacular as we look down on the **Ribeira Brava** basin and across the mountain peaks to **Encumeada** and **Paúl da Serra**.

The path, grassy at first, becomes earthen later and snakes down to arrive at a small forestry house (Wp.11 155M) beside a sharp right hand bend in the road. This area suffered in the Feb 2010 floods, the road surface now resembling a dry waterbed for a short section, though there's no problem with access.

Passing beside terraces with dry stonewalls a narrow *levada* channel runs on our left, fed by a small waterfall. A few minutes along, we pass another waterfall and weir where the overspill washes over the track; note the rare endemic black parsley growing in the hedgerows at this point.

Farm buildings in Fontes

Approaching farm buildings and the first house, the track becomes concrete and descends steeply through a mixture of older and modern property until the lane meets with the regional road in **Fontes** (Wp.12 200M).

Turning right here, **Bar Fontes** is situated on our right in the small square. This is the end of our route and whilst there is a limited bus service, it's probably best to call a taxi to go back to the starting point. The local driver, José Armando, can be reached on 966033815; alternatively, ask at the bar.

2 BOCA DA CORRIDA TO CHÃO DE RELVA AND PICO GRANDE

The **Old Royal Path** is a beautiful mountain trail which crosses part of the central massif and was one the main routes for islanders who moved on horseback between **Corrida** and **Encumeada**. This is **PR12 Caminho Real da Encumeada**, one of the island's official walking trails, but unfortunately due to damage in the Feb 10 floods, the continuous route from **Boca do Cerro** remains closed (September 2011).

Our chosen destination however, takes us along the first four kilometres before making an ascent to the summit of **Pico Grande** and in this wild, mountainous landscape you are likely to spot buzzards, kestrels, firecrests and wagtails.

The route is suitable for most people as far as **Chão de Relva**, but only experienced mountain walkers should consider the final ascent to the summit. There are narrow ledges, with precipitous sections, which could be a problem for vertigo sufferers.

This whole area also suffered severe fire damage in 2010 but recovery has been quite remarkable (May 2011); nevertheless some aspects along the route may vary from our original descriptions.

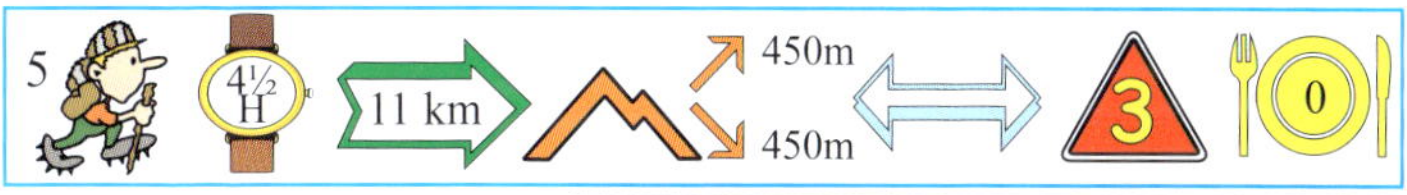

Access by car, taxi or bus: Follow the directions for Walk 1 to **Boca da Corrida**.

São Cristovão Shrine

Starting at the information panel just beyond the **São Cristovão** shrine (Wp.1 0M), we take the railed steps at the side of the panel before ascending a newly laid stairway signed with a fingerpost 'Encumeada'.

The initial 60 metre ascent takes around 10 minutes before we reach a ridge where the path levels out giving us a superb view of **Pico Grande**; standing at 1657 metres, it towers ahead, its rocky castle-like formation on the summit unmistakable. The path crosses the ridge a number of times from east to west passing steep ravines, many bearing small copses of sweet chestnut trees bringing sharp relief to this barren mountainous landscape.

From here on the path undulates, soon passing beside a large rock face (Wp.2 40M) where tree heaths and Echium candicans cling to the sloping hillside Five minutes later we reach a ridge (Wp.3 45M) from where the stony descent to a natural land bridge at **Passo de Ares** can be seen and, after a further ten minutes walking, we cross over this narrow strip, which divides the **Brava** and **Socorridos** river valleys; the views are wonderful (Wp.4 55M).

The view from Boca da Corrida

Continuing on, the path still undulating, we are led around a wide arc at the foot of **Pico do Serradinho**, passing a number of rocky outcrops before circling back westwards to where **Serra da Água** and **Vinháticos** come into view.

Another fifteen minutes and we arrive at **Boca do Cerro** below the impressive **Pico Grande**; the continuing trail to **Encumeada** can now be seen heading west, cutting through dense vegetation at the base of the mountain.

Leaving Corrida

At this point our route leaves the main trail taking a sharp

right hand path indicated with an arrow scratched on a rock (Wp.5 80M) and continues uphill to a red sign where the paths divide; straight ahead leads down to **Nun's Valley**, but we go left to climb past a sheep pen to **Chão de Relva**, a small grassy plateau with a clump of sweet chestnut trees.

Here we have two options, either to rest and soak up the superb views before returning to our starting point or to ascend **Pico Grande**.

To continue on, we climb up above the sheep pens passing another red sign to where a cable is attached to the rock to aid the ascent. Now rising steeply the path, marked with red paint marks and cairns, zigzags

The impressive Pico Grande

up grassy slopes passing through more dense areas of broom and gorse.

On the approach to the summit we are met with the bare rock face and here another cable attached to the rock, aids the final push. The total climb from **Chão de Relva** to the summit is 365 metres over a steep gradient; there are also a number of vertiginous sections, so before continuing, consider your level of fitness and experience as well as your tolerance of vertigo.

Enjoying the views from the summit of Pico Grande (Wp.6)

Those who opt to continue will be rewarded with magnificent views of the mountain range with **Pico Ruivol**, **Pico do Areeiro**, **Nun's Valley** and **Paúl da Serra** displayed from the vantage point on the summit (Wp.6 150M).

After retracing our steps to **Boca da Corrida** (Wp.1 275M) there's a final treat in store for those interested in Portuguese architecture. On the descent from the Forestry House, keep a look out to the right for **Hotel Quinta do Jardim da Serra**, a three-storied pink Mansion House formerly the country estate of Scotsman Henry Veitch; Consul General on the island from 1809-1836, he was also a wine merchant and architect of the Madeira Wine Museum as well as being instrumental in the building of the English church and graveyard in **Funchal**.

Hotel Quinta do Jardim da Serra

This beautiful *quinta* is surrounded by exotic cultivated gardens set against a backdrop of forests and mountains and is well worth a visit.

3 BOCA DOS NAMORADOS - LOMBO CHÃO - NUN'S VALLEY

The *miradouro* at Boca dos Namorados

From this stunning *miradouro* 1050 metres above sea level, you look across to the central massif and down into the great depression of **Curral das Freiras** (Nun's Valley); around its perimeter stand huge eucalyptus and pine trees, with the smaller endemic shrub of Echium candicans (Pride of Madeira) also in abundance.

The walk follows a reasonably good pathway, not too difficult except for one or two unprotected sections which may cause concern for vertigo sufferers. It is not advisable to undertaken this trail in adverse weather conditions, as parts of the path are steep and the surface rocky and often covered in leaf mould.

The continuous route to **Curral das Freiras** is approximately 10kms with a descent of 650 metres and a final ascent of 225 metres. Public transport or taxi is then available for returning to base. Alternatively, this can be done as a 'there and back', turning around at **Lombo Chão**. Walking poles are recommended for both these options.

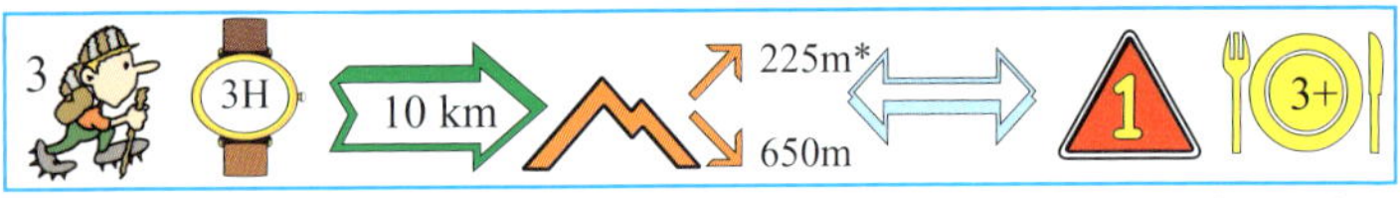

*** excluding the ascent from Corticeiras**

Access by car or taxi:
Follow the ER229 to **Estreito de Cãmara de Lobos**. Turn left beside the church signed 'Jardim da Serra' and continue to climb uphill for a few kilometers. The road to **Boca dos Namorados** is signed off to the right just before the village of **Corticeiras**.

Access by bus:
Bus N°96 serves **Corticeiras**. You then need to take a taxi to the viewpoint or alternatively walk up the old cobbled track or the new road, both of which can be found on the right of the village; the ascent is around 260 metres. Bus N°81 returns to **Funchal** from **Lombo Chão** and **Curral das Freiras**.

After taking in the views (Wp.1 0M), we head towards the far corner of the platform to find a narrow path descending into the woodland. At first this meanders through the trees on a reasonable descent. Seven minutes later, a red painted X appears on a rock and a short distance ahead we are walking beside a large rock wall; as the path underfoot is also solid rock care is needed, particularly in wet or damp conditions.

From this point on our trail passes through sweet chestnut woodland, thoroughly naturalized in this area. Castanea sativa, a member of the Beech family, cultivated both for its appearance and its economic value, is now

Castanea sativa (sweet chestnut)

synonymous with the **Curral Valley**.

With the path becoming steep and zigzagging, we descend sections of rock steps before emerging from the woodland onto the valley side, where amazing vistas of the mountain range and the **Curral Valley** again come into view; here also we enjoy our first sighting of the **Pico do Cedro** plateau with its electricity pylon.

.. amazing vistas..

The path continues along a wide ledge with a deep valley to our right and care is again needed along this short section. With more rocky steps and zigzagging, we now get a glimpse of the river in the bottom of the valley before re-entering the woodland on the approach to **Pico do Cedro**.

Soon arriving on the plateau (Wp.2 40M) we find ourselves surrounded by bracken, laurels and chestnuts; from this vantage point we take in our first views of **Lombo Chão** and the road below the settlement leading to the valley floor.

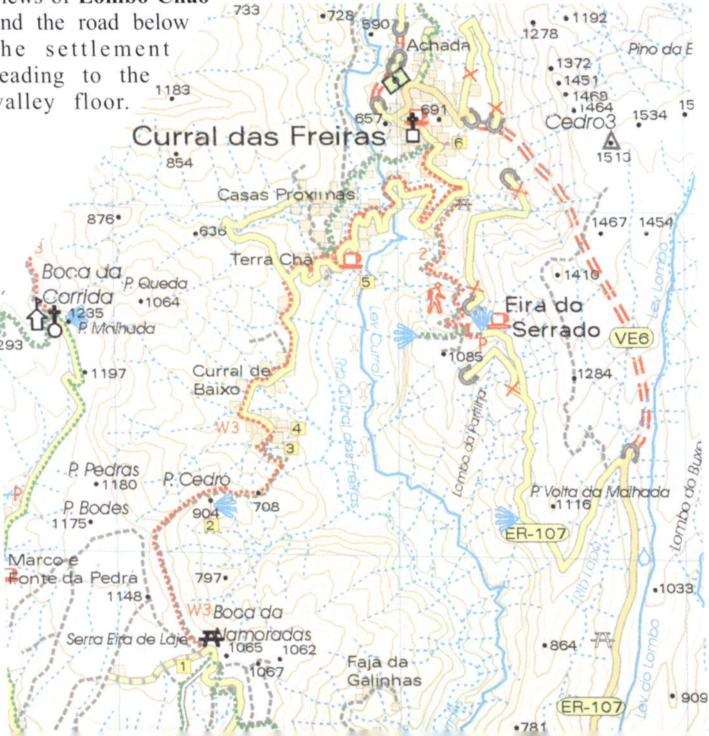

Leaving **Pico do Cedro**, the path again descends steeply, becoming rocky underfoot before levelling out for a brief section as we head into a wooded side valley; for a short distance we are now heading in a southerly direction behind a rocky cliff.

From here the path is good and wide with rock steps twisting and turning down through the forest; the conditions becoming much damper here, providing an ideal habitat for the ferns, lichens and mosses which adorn the rocky walls. Log steps ease our descent, before we arrive at a paved section of path which we assume leads us down to the settlement, but for some reason this soon becomes an earthen forest track again.

Morning Glory (Convolvulaceae)

Approaching **Lombo Chão**, we hear the sound of running water and after a few minutes, cross the watercourse on stepping-stones (Wp.3 115M). Here Morning Glory (Convolvulaceae) covers the hedgerows as we make a short ascent to arrive at the first house of the settlement.

At the junction just beyond the house we then turn left to ascend a flight of steps, arriving at the bus shelter and turning circle (Wp.4 120M). We follow the **Estrada do Lombo Chão** out of the village and after a short ascent, ignoring a road off to our right, we continue along for a total of 1.8kms to reach **Ribeira Curral das Freiras** in the valley bottom (Wp.5 140M).

The first bar in the village (Wp.6)

Crossing over the bridge, the road begins a steady climb for 2.4kms, before arriving at the first bar and bus stop just below the village centre (Wp.6 180M).

Curral das Freiras is a traditional rural settlement founded in the 1566 by the nuns of the **Convent of Santa Clara** who fled from **Funchal** following an attack by pirates. Seeking permanent refuge here, the sisters erected the first church in the area and created the agricultural environment which remains today. The village has a thriving centre relying mainly on tourism, hosting the Chestnut Festival each November which draws in tourists and local people from across the island. Village specialties of chestnut soup, bread and cakes and chestnut liquor are offered in the shops and restaurants around the village.

4 LEVADA DO NORTE - ESTREITO DE CÃMARA DE LOBOS to CABO GIRÃO

Cabo Girão is the second highest sea cliff in Europe, rising 580m above sea level. Far below the spectacular viewpoint you can see the minute plots of land where vines grow below the sunny cliffs.

For much of the route we find ourselves passing between houses and vineyards, vines shading our way and stretching out before us like a patchwork; this is the area that produces the grapes for Madeira wine. The route also passes through cherry orchards, beautiful in late spring, before entering into a deeply wooded valley where the valley heads are crossed on two bridges before continuing south to **Cabo Girão**.

At the twenty-minute point there is a detour below the channel to avoid an extremely narrow section cut into the valley side. This occurs immediately following a right hand bend, so make sure you look out for the alternative path dropping below the channel. There are also a few short precipitous sections a little further along, where care is needed.

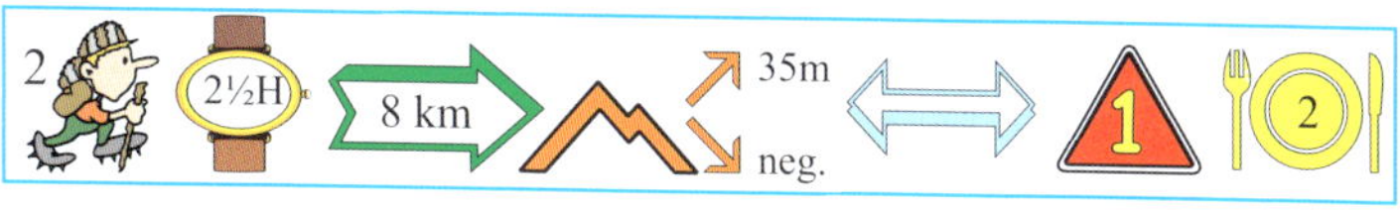

Access by car or taxi:
Follow the ER229 to the centre of **Estreito de Cãmara de Lobos**, turning left immediately after the church signed 'Jardim da Serra'. The *levada* crosses over the road approximately 600m ahead.

Access by bus:
Take bus Nº96 from **Funchal** via **Estreito de Cãmara de Lobos** alighting at the **Levada do Norde** bus stop. Return from **Cruz da Caldeira** (close to **Cabo Girão**) to **Estreito** or **Funchal** on bus Nº154.

The start of the walk

We pick up the *levada* on the left side of the road where a large sign 'Levada do Norte' directs us along a pink paved pathway under the vines (Wp.1 0M). Soon crossing a small bridge at a valley head then passing beside more houses and agricultural plots, we meet a tarred road where the channel is culverted; it is picked up again around 300m ahead.

With houses and vineyards scattered across the hillside, the trail heads into a deeply wooded valley where after around twenty minutes walking, the *levada* suddenly sweeps to the right (Wp.2 20M).

Entering the deep valley

Here the concrete shoulder becomes extremely narrow passing under overhanging rock, so our route follows a detour below the channel rejoining it again a short distance ahead.

This beautiful valley, rich in flora, is extremely deep and the *levada* again becoming precipitous on a couple of sections. Here the rock overhangs the channel and we must stoop to pass by so caution is needed at this point.

Nevertheless, easy walking follows and a short distance ahead we cross a bridge over a deep gorge, the river tumbling down waterfalls on our right before dropping into the gorge below (Wp.3 35M).

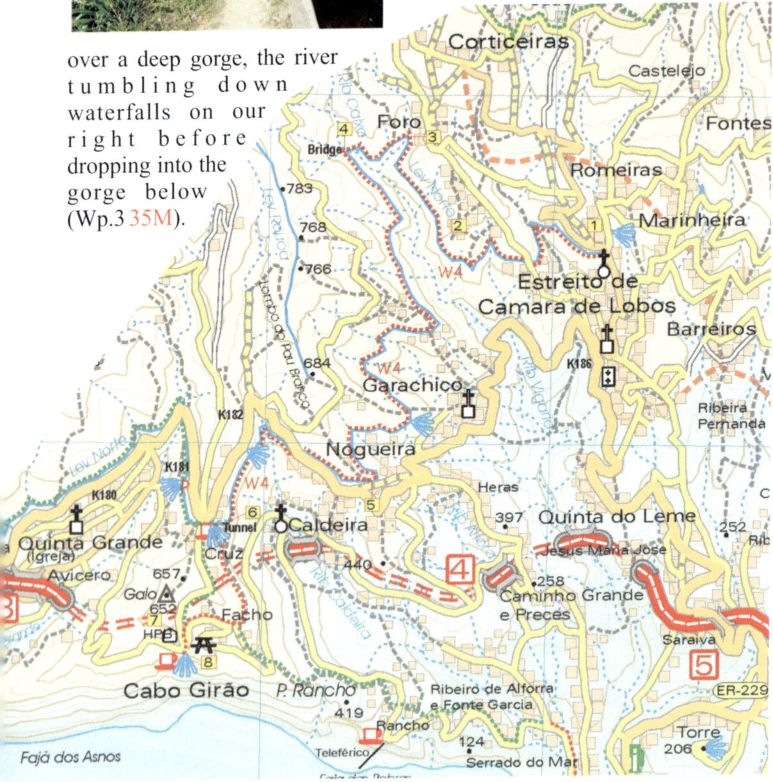

Now circling below the settlements of **Jardim da Serra** we arrive at a second river where a new iron bridge has been erected (Wp.4 50M). Crossing over, our route heads out of the valley towards the village of **Garachico**.

The next section is quite long and on our survey (Mar 2011) there was still evidence of damage from the Feb 2010 floods. However, the wonderful views compensate and from hereon we look across to the coastline and over to the **Desertas Islands** with the vast patchwork of vineyards stretching out before us down the deep valley.

On arriving in **Garachico**, the channel is mostly covered, often becoming the village street; a few minutes along it disappears and is picked up again by crossing diagonally over the road. Heading round a rocky section below the road, water emerges from a tunnel on our right.

A few minutes later, after crossing in front of some houses, the channel reaches another dead end at a water station and here our route drops down a stepped slope to meet a cobbled lane (Wp.5 105M). Turning right and passing a water tank on our right, the *levada* is rejoined around 30m ahead on the opposite side of the lane.

Levada do Norte

Five minutes later the route crosses a large earthen area where in the past the hillside has fallen away obliterating the channel. This section is well signed but the red clay can be slippery when wet. Arriving at a waterfall at the final valley head there is evidence again of flood damage but whilst the crossing is a little tricky, it's quite safe, albeit you may get a little wet.

Contouring along the western edge of the valley, the next section of the channel has been rebuilt and soon the *levada* makes a right turn to enter a tunnel (Wp.6 125M) that's around 300m long, leading to the far side of **Cabo Girão**.

We leave **Levada do Norte** at this point, now continuing straight ahead to follow the smaller *levada* signed 'Vereda Levada do Facho'. We're now passing through the settlement of **Nogueira**, the new road from the Holiday Property Bond Timeshare Complex seen below us on our left.

Around ten minutes after crossing over a steep stepped pathway, **Levada do Facho** comes to an end and here steps lead up right to join the road in the HPB complex (Wp.7 140M). Turning right, our route now ascends the road between the reception building and apartment blocks to reach the **Cabo Girão** *miradouro* and facilities (Wp.8 150M).

View east to Câmara de Lobos and Funchal

The viewpoint, road network and visitor facilities are currently being redeveloped (March 2011) but the area remains open and is bustling with tourists. After enjoying the views and the atmosphere at this spectacular cliff top, we can either retrace our steps back to the starting point, or take a taxi or bus back to base.

There's a taxi stand close to the *miradouro* and the bus stop can be found a short distance along the road at **Cruz da Caldeira**.

5 LEVADA DO NORTE from BOA MORTE to EIRA DO MOURÃO & ESPIGÃO

This trail has all the ingredients for an exciting and challenging walk with wonderful views, varied flora and remote village settings. There are tunnels and caves en-route and also the option to make a spectacular descent to the settlement of **Fajá da Ribeira** in **Ribeira Brava**. Following **Levada do Norte** to **Espigão**, we have a reasonably easy stroll along the first section as far as **Eira do Mourão**; thereafter the channel shoulder becomes increasingly exposed and precipitous, so a head for heights and sure-footedness are absolutely essential beyond this point. Less experienced walkers or those suffering from vertigo may wish to turn around here and return to the starting point or alternatively make the descent to **Fajã da Ribeira**.

Periwinkle

Boa Morte is the start and finish point for both versions of this walk with the optional descent ending in **Ribeira Brava**, both providing lots of wonderful aspects to take our interest, the vegetation becoming more wilder as we progress. Sweet Chestnuts abound while around the settlements indigenous flora is interspersed with the exotic; carpets of Bermuda buttercups, mallow, valerian and periwinkle mingle with globularia, prickly pear and houseleeks.

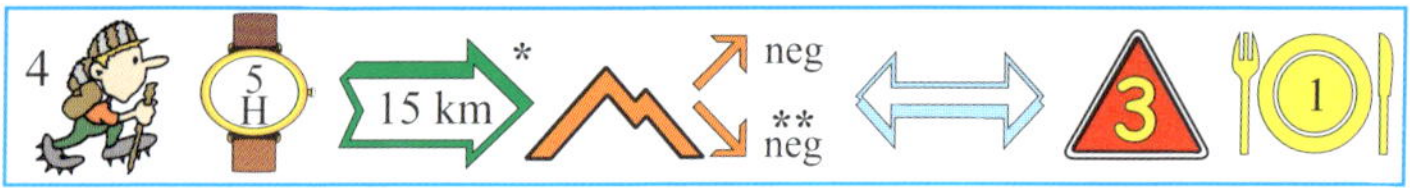

* shorter version 8km ** optional descent to **Fajã da Ribeira** 460m

Access by car or taxi:
Take junction 2 from the VR1 (**Via Rápida**) and follow the signs for 'Campanário', keeping left at two junctions. Approximately 1km from the Rápida, take a road on the right signed 'São Pedro', 'Boa Morte', 'Lugar da Serra' and 'Parque Empresario'. This new section of road passes through two tunnels before reaching the industrial park roundabout. Turn left for **Boa Morte**; the *levada* crosses the road about 50 metres from the junction. Parking is available a further 150 metres along the road beside **O Pinheiro Snack Bar**.

Access by bus:
Rodoeste bus Nº127 from **Ribeira Brava** serves **Boa Morte** and **Fontes** or take Nº148 from **Funchal** to **Boa Morte** via **Cãmara de Lobos** & **Campanário**.

Our route begins around 40 metres above the bar, where 'Levada do Norte' is signed and crosses the road (Wp.1 0M). Going left, we follow the channel upstream as it cuts through a dense stand of pine. After passing beside a huge concrete wall to our right, we emerge onto the eastern slopes of the **Ribeira Brava** basin to fine views along the valley.

Dipping in and out of pine and eucalyptus woodland, we pass beside a water pumping station (Wp.2 20M), our path becoming more exposed but not dangerous as there's lots of vegetation.

The channel curves to the right as it runs into a side valley; a little further along another channel feeds into the *levada* (Wp.3 35M); we find ourselves at the valley head and cross a bridge above the deep gorge of **Ribeira Funda** from which the surrounding village takes its name (Wp.4 40M). Houses spill down the hillside; many close to the *levada* are abandoned although the hamlet is not deserted and there's still plenty of activity to be seen on the surrounding agricultural terraces. There's an abundance of Sweet Chestnut trees as well as oranges, tropical fruits and vines and we are likely to meet the occasional tethered goat along the pathway. Leaving **Ribeira Funda** behind, the *levada* sweeps back again towards the main valley.

Looking down on Eira do Mourão

As we veer right, the tiny settlement of **Eira do Mourão** comes into view. This pretty hamlet nestles precariously on a rocky mountain ridge; as we cross over the tarred access road (Wp.5 55M) we can pick out the 2000 steps zigzagging down into the valley. This is the optional route to **Fajã da Ribeira**.

Here we make a choice; our main route continues along the *levada* towards **Espigão** but with some exposed and precipitous sections, particularly after the tunnel. Our shorter option is to drop down the road to the hamlet, taking in spectacular views of the surrounding valleys and peaks, before either returning by the same route to the starting point or taking the steps down to **Fajá** (see directions below).

Our main route continues along the *levada* following a high ridge along the mountainside. We pass beside a pretty water house, enjoying good views across **Serra da Água** and **Encumeada** before veering right into the vast valley of **Ribeira Espigão,** its extreme slopes sculpted with agricultural terraces sprawling below us, the plantations across the valley dotted with numerous beehives.

Passing beside the waterhouse

Initially the path is quite wide and comfortable but becomes much more exposed and vertiginous as we progress. We pass through a narrow cutting (Wp.6 85M) before reaching a short tunnel carved through a huge rock with an interesting cave above it (Wp.7 90M).

The first short tunnel and cave (Wp.7)

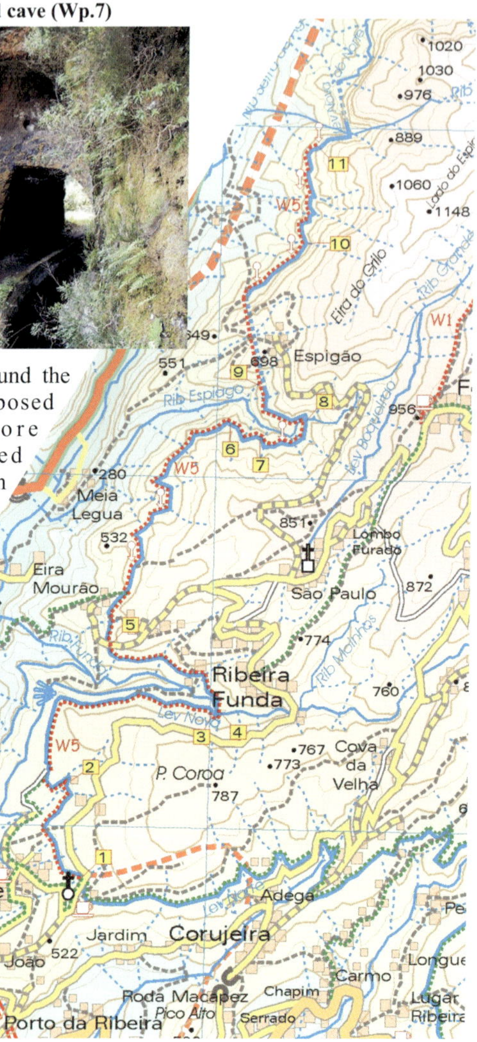

The channel swings round the valley, crossing exposed sections, then more comfortable wooded stretches but there's often overhanging rock with water dripping down from above (Wp.8 100M).

As we go through deeper vegetation, we arrive at a waterfall and a tunnel entrance covered in ferns (Wp.9 110M). The tunnel, around 100m long, passes under the village of **Espigão** and takes around ten minutes to walk through.

The exposed section

The tunnel path is occasionally wet and muddy, but there is a wall between the channel and path and plenty of headroom; however, a torch is needed.

On emerging from the darkness we are greeted with lush green vegetation though at this point the path narrows considerably and becomes extremely precipitous, requiring our undivided attention along the remainder of the route.

The exposure along this final section is quite awesome as the channel passes through a rock cutting with rivulets and overhangs, often making progress more difficult (Wp.10 130M), but with the reward of brilliant views (remembering to stop before looking) across to **Encumeada**, **Serra da Água** and the mountain peaks.

Around 20 minutes after leaving the **Espigão** tunnel, we find a number of 'Red Danger' crosses painted on the rocks and shortly after the channel sweeps right (Wp.11 140M). From here on the route becomes extremely dangerous so we go no further, though standing at this point, we can look ahead to see the *levada* crossing the vertical rock face and just after a large waterfall, entering another tunnel.
On no account should we progress along this section. Shortly after these red danger markers, we must retrace our steps back to our starting point (Wp.1 300M) or as far as **Eira do Mourão** (Wp.5 230M) to make the descent to **Fajã** and **Ribeira Brava**.

Optional descent to Fajã da Ribeira (Descent 460m - Allow 1 hour)

Cave house on the optional descent

Back at **Eira do Mourão** (Wp.5), we descend the tarred access road leading into the parking bay and head for steps leading off left at the side of a newly renovated house. This trail down to **Fajã** is quite spectacular, although rather challenging, especially the first very steep section.

After crossing a bridge over the **Ribeira Funda** our route turns right and becomes easier as we follow a narrow *levada*. The vegetation is dense here and there are a few derelict cottages around, a legacy to the humble and difficult life of earlier settlers in this area.

6 LEVADA DO NORTE AND LEVADA DAS RABAÇAS - ENCUMEADA

Boca da Encumeada (1007m) sits at the head of a great rift, dividing the island at an almost central point. The highest peaks lie to the east with the plateau of **Paúl da Serra** to the west. From the viewpoint on the summit, both north and south coastlines are visible; it's best to go there in the morning as later in the day blankets of cloud can drape the summit obliterating these stunning views.

The view east to Pico Grande

The ER105 regional highway climbing from **Ribeira Brava** and over the **Encumeada Pass**, as well as the ER228 which drops down into **São Vicente**, are two of the most scenic routes on the island, making **Boca da Encumeada** a vibrant centre for tourists and hikers.

Our short trail follows **Levada do Norte** and **Levada das Rabaças** along the southern mountain slopes above **Ribeira Brava**, the pathway, bordered with exotic flora, allowing stunning views along its whole length.

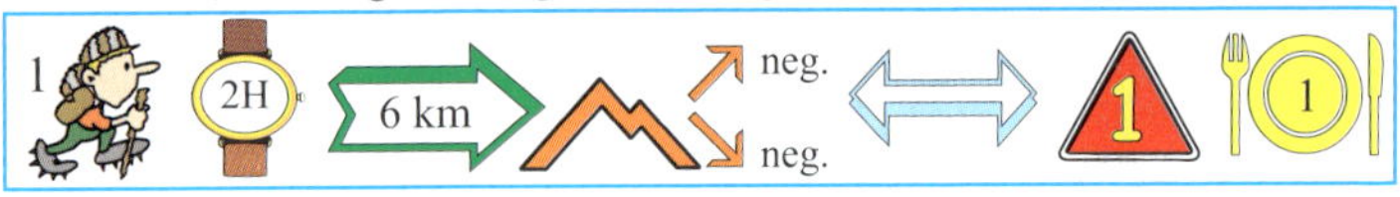

Access by hire car or taxi:
Take the VE4 north from **Ribeira Brava**, turning left on the ER105 for **Serra da Agua** and **Encumeada**. **Snack Bar Encumeada** is located on the right of the road as you approach the summit. From the west, approach via the **Paúl da Serra** crossroads, taking the ER105 east for 12 kms through **Encumeada** pass and turning right after the gift shop signed 'Ribeira Brava'. The snack bar is located a few metres below the junction.

Access by bus:
Rodoeste routes Nºs 6 and 139 from **Funchal** and **Ribeira Brava** serve **Boca da Encumeada**.

Setting off

Across from the **Encumeada Snack Bar** a short flight of steps lead us up to an information panel on the shoulder of **Levada do Norte** (Wp.1 0M). This indicates the route for the **PR17 Caminho do Pináculo e Folhadal**, which we follow for a short distance before heading off onto **Levada das Rabaças**.

Following the channel upstream along a substantial path, our route is bordered with Agapanthus (Lily of the Nile) and Hydrangea. Soon we pass beside the water keeper's house, a pretty building surrounded by lush vegetation; a water separation point is negotiated a little further ahead.

.. Residential Encumeada nestles below ..

Splendid views open up along the route looking down on the **Ribeira Brava** valley and east to **Pico Grande**, soon after arriving at a *miradouro* (Wp.2 18M) from where the **Residencial Encumeada Hotel** is seen nestling on the slopes below us.

Levada das Rabaças

The path loops along the slopes passing through woodland of Laurel, Conifer, Oak, Cedar and Beech with endemic Echium candican, Melliferous spurge and Globularia also appearing.

We arrive at a tunnel entrance on our right (Wp.3 20M) where our trail leaves the PR17 route, the latter heading off through the tunnel. Our route continues ahead following **Levada das Rabaças**, the vegetation soon thinning out so opening up vistas all around. South is **Serra da Água** and ahead, magnificent peaks appear.

The trail passes beside a large rock fall and later makes a short detour below a huge rock (Wp.4 43M), scars from the 2010 floods though the *levada* and shoulder have been reconstructed and made safe.

Approaching the end of the route

As the peaks tower ahead of us, a few narrow sections of channel follow which are mildly precipitous, before we arrive at a large valley head with waterfalls to our right. Again much reconstruction has been undertaken here, these works in no way detracting from the magnificence of the scenery around us.

Arriving at a tunnel entrance (Wp.5 55M) the walk comes to an end and from here we retrace our steps back to the starting point, enjoying the different perspective of the return journey (Wp.1 110M).

Extension (Total route 12 kms - 4 hrs one-way)

Levada das Rabaças enters the tunnel at Wp.5 making a continuous route under the **Encumeada Pass** to reach the **Cristo Rio** statue on the ER209 below **Paúl da Serra**. Whilst this is a superb trail it is quite challenging, negotiating two tunnels 200m and 3kms in length, both easily passable with care. At this point the trail arrives at **Cascalho**, a spectacular amphitheatre at the head of the **Ponta da Sol** valley before making a 350m ascent along an earthen track to arrive on **Levada da Bica da Cana**. The route then links with Walk 27 coming in from the opposite direction.

This continuous route was closed in 2010 for repair work, so anyone wishing to walk on to **Cristo Rei** should first contact the tourist offices or speak with the *lavadeiros* at the **Encumeada** water house, to check the status of the trail before setting out.

7 MONTE - BOM SUCESSO - FUNCHAL

This trail explores the deep gorge between **Monte** and the **Botanical Gardens**, before leading us under the **Via Rápida** bridge to make a final descent to the sea front of **Funchal**.

The path through the woods is very steep in places and care is needed with the steps. Along the route, we also follow **Levada do Bom Sucesso**, which has a few tricky and precipitous sections.

Nevertheless this is a superb walk, which can be made into a circular by taking the *teleférico* from **Old Town** to **Monte** and also makes a memorable day out if we combine our walk with a visit to the historic centre of **Monte**, with its tropical gardens, impressive church, toboggan run, and lovely squares.

Our Lady of Monte church

The toboggans

This route was closed following the February 2010 floods and repair work was still ongoing at the time of writing (May 2011). Being a privately owned *levada*, it's been more difficult to track but we are advised that the trail will reopen again in the coming months. Therefore please check the status of the route with the tourist offices before setting out.

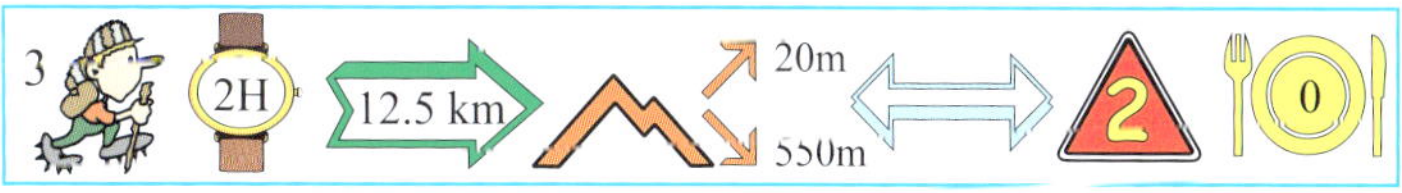

Access by car hire or taxi:
Follow the ER103 from Funchal to **Monte**. The main car park is situated just above the village.

Access by bus:
Town Buses N°s 20, 21 & 48 serve **Monte**. Alternatively take the *teleférico* for a spectacular ascent from **Funchal** seafront.

The route starts in **Babosas** square; situated just below the **Funchal** *teleférico* terminus (Wp.1 0M). Here we take the

The cable car station

cobbled lane down into the valley, passing the cable car station for the **Botanical Gardens**, to arrive at a junction where the path to **Levada dos Tornos** is signed off left (Wp.2 12M).

Descending to the Botanical Gardens

Our route continues down the cobbled path to the right, signed as **Levada do Bom Sucesso**. After crossing the pretty stone bridge over the **Ribeira de João Gomes** (Wp.3) we climb up to a path junction where **Curral dos Romeiros** is signed to the left and **Levada do Bom Sucesso** to the right (Wp.4 22M).

We turn right off the main track and drop down the eastern side of the valley on a log-stepped descent, with the remains of rustic handrails lining the woodland path in places. This is such an attractive route and looking across to our right we can see the *teleférico* on it's spectacular route above the tree canopy.

A particularly steep zigzag (Wp.5 30M) brings us to a flat clearing before we continue down through the forest on wooden steps, churning river sounds rising from the rocky watercourse below. Passing evidence of an old wall, we come to a T-junction, where going right will take us to a waterfall, while our onward route goes left here.

Our path levels out for a section, passing a cave on the left (Wp.6) before descending again alongside the steep gorge with its rushing water. Another steep descent (46M) brings us close to the river before we cross a rock-filled gully (Wp.7) to contour along the valley wall in gentle descents. The impressive **Via Rápida** bridge, now dominates the view ahead.

A red and yellow waymark (Wp.8) confirms our route just before a junction with a path climbing up to our left; this leads to **Curral dos Romeiros**, though the signpost no longer exists. We come across a small area where large Agaves adorn our route, perhaps escapes from the **Botanical Gardens**.

.. large Agaves adorn our route ..

At the next faint path junction at the bottom of a flight of steps (Wp.9) we keep right, to descend beside flimsy guard rails before passing log steps which climb up to the left and then stone steps. A wire guard rail bring us down to a stone bridge (Wp.10 68M) at the start of the **Levada do Bom Sucesso**. This narrow but fast flowing *levada* marks the end of the woodland descent.

The tricky section at Wp.12

Following it, we edge round a rock face to walk above sheer drops before reaching a less vertiginous section (Wp.11) facing the **Via Rápida** bridge. We curve into a small side valley beneath the remains of a substantial house, then cross an aqueduct bridge on stepping stones between rocks, which needs very careful footwork as some of the slabs are missing (Wp.12).

Coming out of the valley, we are hit by traffic noise as we stroll along to pass under the **Via Rápida** (Wp.13 87M), our path running below the *levada* for a short section before coming back onto its wall; the houses of **Bom Sucesso** now come into view.

As we pass the first house, we come to the end of the tarmaced **Rua Antonio Costa Medico** (Wp.14), to take a pedestrian stairway down to our right. Descending between tight-packed houses, we reach a tarmac road (Wp.15 102M); crossing carefully, we go onto the **João Gomez** walkway to continue dropping down through the houses, passing walkways off to our left. More walkways branch off the main route as we continue steeply down to emerge from the **Travesa de Ribeira João Gomes** onto the pavement by the main road (Wp.16 107M).

Turning downhill, we stroll down pavements and across a tiny square, the road becoming fully commercialized, before we reach our finish at the taxi rank (Wp.17 121M) just before the sea front in **Funchal**.

8 PICO DO AREEIRO - JUNCAL VIEWPOINT - NINHO DA MANTA

The route to Ruivo

Pico do Areeiro (1817m) is the start point for the **PR1 Vereda do Areeiro**, one of the island's most popular high altitude trails linking this peak with **Ruivo** (1862m), highest point on the island. The area around the summit has changed significantly over the last couple of years; a military radar station and reception building now dominate the adjacent area but don't detract too much from this spectacular mountain region.

Echium candicans

Our short alternative trail provides an opportunity for everyone to enjoy walking a section of the **Areeiro** - **Ruivo** route as far as **Ninho da Manta**. It also takes in another short trail east, to the **Juncal** viewpoint overlooking the northern slopes and coastline.

Pico do Areeiro is an important area for flora and fauna and is the only known breeding site in the world of the Zino's Petrel, Europe's rarest seabird and one of the rarest in the world; there are said to be between 65 and 80 pairs in this location.

There's a wealth of rare high altitude flora; in summer Madeira thrift, chrysanthemums, hawkweed, kidney vetch, Echium candicans and rock mustard abound whilst rarer endemics such as Madeira eyebright, Madeira saxifrage, Madeira violets, and stonecrops cling to rock face crevices and ledges. The area sits close to the northern boundary of the **Funchal Ecological Park**, another important area of the national park; see footnote.

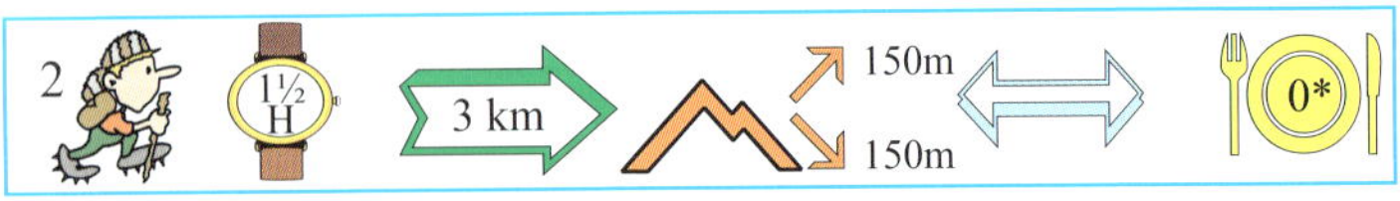

Access by car hire or taxi:
Follow the ER103 from **Funchal** via **Monte** and continue on to **Poiso**. At the road junction just beyond the **Abrigo do Poiso Restaurant**, go left on the ER202. It's around 7km to the car park at **Pico do Areeiro**.

Leaving the car park (Wp.1 0M) and passing around the left side of the building, we take steps up to the back terrace and follow the first section of the disabled access route to reach a paved pathway leading down to a turning

On the path to Juncal

circle at the gates to the radar station. On the opposite side of the road at a break in the wall (Wp.2), our trail continues along an old cobbled path, making a short initial ascent before passing around a rocky outcrop and descending.

Ignoring two paths off to the left, we reach a few steps before our route turns right and then left to reach the fenced platform of the *miradouro* (Wp.3 10M).

From here there are fine views of the deep-forested valley of **Fajã da Nogueira** as well as the villages of **São Roque** and **Faial** and of **Penha de Águia** (Eagle Rock) on the north coast. The hydropower station at **Fajã da Nogueira** can be seen deep in the valley, as can the *levadas* that feed the station which provides water for the northern settlements.

Retracing our steps and heading back towards the summit of **Areeiro**, the trail picks up the disabled access as it zig-zags up to a junction; the path to **Ninho da Manta** (Wp.4 30M) leads off left here, steps to the peak go right. At the top of the steps go left to follow a circular path clockwise, soon taking another short flight of steps to the summit (Wp.5 35M). After soaking up the magnificent views we return to Wp.4 to follow the paved walkway of **PR1** across the narrow saddle of a vast rocky area, our path making a steep descent down many steps before reaching a wide grassy area.

There are magnificent views all around with the main route to **Ruivo** seen continuing along the mountain range below **Pico das Torrres**. From the grassy area there's a short ascent before dropping again to the foot of a huge rocky outcrop on top of which sits the **Ninho da Manta** *miradouro*. Climbing steps beside the rock face, the **PR1** trail to **Ruivo** ascends left, while our trail turns right to reach the viewpoint (Wp.6 60M). We retrace our steps back to the car park (Wp.1 90M).

Ninho da Manta

As there is no public transport to **Pico do Areeiro** you will need to travel by hire car, taxi or tour bus, but whichever mode of transport you chose, try to arrange to stop at the **Poço da Neve** (Snow House) on your return journey. Also known as the **Ice House**, it is situated on the right of the ER202 about 2 kilometres from the summit car park.

Poço da Neve

Built by Madeiran stonemasons and financed by an Italian ice-cream maker, the **Ice House** provided ice for hospitals and Reid's Hotel from 1813 until the end of the nineteenth century. Access to this amazing monument is by a narrow paved path leading from the road across the moorland.

Funchal Ecological Park

The **Ice House** stands on the northern boundary of the **Funchal Ecological Park**, which occupies an area of around 1000 hectares, extending from the forested areas above **Funchal** to **Pico Areeiro**. Unfortunately the park suffered severe damage from the August 2010 fires with ninety-five percent of its area being affected. But nature is a great healer; ground cover and low vegetation again flourish and a restoration programme is in place for rapid replanting and tree clearance.

In spite of this disaster, the park remains popular with visitors; the gardens surrounding the **Ecological Park Reception Centre** at **Ribeira das Cales** have been spared and still look marvellous. Here you'll find an information centre and café as well as the nursery raising endemic species for the replanting programme.

Ecological Park Reception Centre

Within the park there are picnic and barbeque facilities as well as the donkeys, currently stabled at **Casa do Burro** higher up the park; sadly since the fires, these have been unavailable for park excursions.

There are three official walking routes, two starting from the Ice House and descending the length of the park and one from the **Ecological Park Reception Centre** to **Monte** - all of which intersect with the ornithological routes. Unfortunately the two longer trails and the bird watching routes are not recommended at the moment, but plans are in place for re-signage in 2012. The shorter route to **Monte** remains open. The walking trails are summarized as follows:

PR3.1 - Caminho Real do Monte

This lovely walk descends 2 kilometres through the park before continuing on an ancient trail originally linking settlements in the north and south. At around the halfway point the path emerges onto the regional road beside **Quinta Terreiro da Luta**; originally built as a rail station, it's now a restaurant surrounded by beautiful gardens. There's also an opportunity at this point to visit the statue of **Our Lady of Peace** situated close by. The final section down to **Monte** descends a leafy lane passing the Stations of the Cross before arriving at **Monte** botanical gardens and the famous church of **Nossa Senhora do Monte**.

The donkeys (in their original stables)

PR3 -Vereda do Burro

The next two trails start at **Poço da Neve**, this one leading over **Pico dos Melros** to reach the recreational area around **Casa do Burro** at **Chão da Lagoa**, the area where the donkeys are temporarily housed. This central trail then continues on to the reception centre at **Ribeira das Cales**.

PR4 - Levada do Barreiro

The final route leaves the **Ice House** to descend the easterly ridge of the **Ribeira de Santa Luzia** valley providing spectacular views along the way. Following **Levada do Barreiro**, the trail drops down to **Casa do Barreiro** in the south of the park before climbing back to end at **Ribeira das Cales**.

The full walking notes for these three routes are included in Walk! Madeira and shown on the Madeira Tour & Trail map, both published by Discovery Walking Guides.

9 SANTANA - PICO DAS PEDRAS to QUEIMADAS

traditional A-framed cottage

The north coastal town of **Santana** comprises the parishes of **Arco de São Jorge, São Jorge, Ilha, Faial** and **São Roque do Faial**. An area rich in culture, it's famous for wine-making, traditional folklore and the pretty A-framed thatched cottages found scattered across the landscape. In addition it now hosts the new **Madeira Theme Park**. Some of the best walking routes on the island are accessed from **Santana**, the pathway to **Pico Ruivo** (the highest peak at 1862m) is only around 4 kilometres up the ER218, plus there are a number of other high altitude routes and coastal pathways close by. (See footnotes for further information)

This trail takes us from **Rancho** in the **Pico das Pedras** forestry park to **Casa de Abrigo das Queimadas**, the most beautiful forestry house estate on the island and the starting point of the official **PR9 Levada do Caldeirão Verde**. A gentle stroll through a tranquil area of natural and exotic forest, it's extremely popular with visitors; it's also designated as a suitable trail for disabled and blind walkers. At **Rancho** there's a snack bar as well as accommodation in the *colmos*, the traditional triangular shaped houses with thatched roofs.

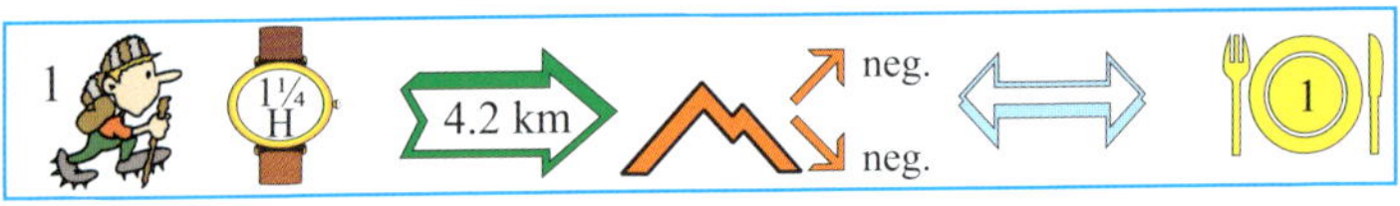

Access by car or taxi:
Take the ER213 east from **Santana**, turning right after one kilometre onto the ER218, signed 'Achada do Teixeira'. The car park for **Rancho**, **Pico das Pedras** is located on the right of the road around 4 kilometres from the junction with the ER213. There is a large car park off the road with additional parking beside the snack bar.

Access by bus:
There is a regular bus service (Route N°s 56, 103 & 138) from **Funchal** to **Santana** from where taxis are available to deliver you to the starting point at **Rancho** car park, **Pico das Pedras**.

Forest path from Pico das Pedras

Leaving the car park (Wp.1 0M) and passing beside traditional houses, we enter the woodland, our pathway flanked with agapanthus and hydrangea and fenced throughout. Soon we pick up the **Levada do Caldeirão Verde** running on our left and follow it upstream. A few minutes along it crosses over to the right (Wp.2 5M), from whereon the channel meanders back and forth across the broad tree-shaded trail. Deciduous oaks, beech and sycamore line our route alongside laurels and conifers, the latter including some splendid cedars - occasionally splashes of colour also appear from the introduced camellias and azaleas.

Anemone-leaved crane's bill

We swing into a deeper valley, crossing the watercourse at its head (Wp.3 15M), our route soft and cushioned underfoot. Woodland flowers appear alongside the path; there are anemone-leaved crane's bill and Canary buttercups in abundance and the rare musschia wollastonii can also be spotted here. Large patches of fungus grow on a maple tree to our left just before we arrive at a rushing stream, which we cross on a concrete bridge (Wp.4 30M). A few minutes later we leave the trail, stepping onto the cobbled access lane to **Parque das Queimadas** a cobbled lane coming up on our right (Wp.5 35M). Crossing over, we enter into this wonderful estate situated above the agricultural lands of **Santana**.

Canary buttercups

The forestry house, with original features of the typical houses in this region, has a marvellous thatched roof as does another smaller building close by and even the ducks have been provided with their own thatched houses on the banks of the two lovely ponds.

The paved courtyard is surrounded by elegant parkland with excellent specimens of Japanese Cedars and European Beech as well as magnificent displays of rhododendrons. You'll also find tame chaffinches hopping around the picnic area looking for scraps; it's a wonderful area and worthy of a visit in its own right.

This is the end of our trail and from here we can either retrace our steps back to the starting point at **Rancho** (Wp.1 75M) or, extend the walk along **Levada do Caldeirão Verde (PR9)**. This well-known 6.5km trail (one way) is signed just beyond the house, taking us through the *laurisilva* into the interior. With spectacular views of the mountainous terrain along the way, it also passes through four tunnels before arriving at a huge basin with towering walls and here the **Caldeirão Verde** stream falls 100 metres into a lovely green lake. (See Walk! Madeira for the full walking notes on this route).

Casa de Abrigo das Queimadas

Chaffinch

Additional official walking routes around Santana:

PR1.2 Vereda do Pico Ruivo

This route begins around 4km above **Pico das Pedras** at **Achada do Teixeira** and provides a spectacular walk along a comfortable paved pathway with no precipitous drops. Refreshments are available at the government shelter below the summit. (6km return - Allow 2¼ hrs return)

PR1.1 Vereda da Ilha

Starting at the 30 minute point along the **Ruivo** pathway, this trail descends 1215m to the parish of **Ilha** above **São Jorge**. (10.5km one-way - Allow 4 hours from the starting point)

PR1 Vereda do Areeiro

The most popular high altitude route on the island, this trail crosses the central massif on a spectacular journey joining two of the highest peaks, **Ruivo** and **Areeiro**. (10 km one-way from **Teixeira** - Allow 4hrs)

PR1.3 Vereda da Encumeada

Starting at the government shelter below **Ruivo** summit, this trail crosses the central mountains in a westerly direction to reach **Boca da Encumeada**. (14km one-way - Allow 5hrs)

PR18 Levada do Rei

Starting at **Quebrados** in **São Jorge**, the channel flows through a spectacular area of natural forest to its source in the riverbed of the **Ribeiro Bonito** (beautiful river). (10.2km return - Allow 3½ hrs)

Full walking instructions for all these official PR routes are included in the 2nd and 3rd editions of Walk! Madeira. Two of **Santana**'s beautiful coastal trails are included in this publication - see Walks 15 & 16.

10 ABRIGO DO PASTOR CIRCULAR

Abrigo do Pastor

This beautiful short circular walk starts and ends at **Abrigo do Pastor** (Shepherd's Rest), one of the best rural hostelries on the island. On walking into this charming establishment, you could be forgiven for thinking you are entering an English country pub, complete with open fire, wooden beams and a warm inviting atmosphere.

The walk takes us along ancient routes through forested vales and hills dotted with farming hamlets, before leading us into Madeira's main sheep farming area where unusual breeds, adorned with tinkling bells, roam in an idyllic setting of rolling moorland and deciduous woodland.

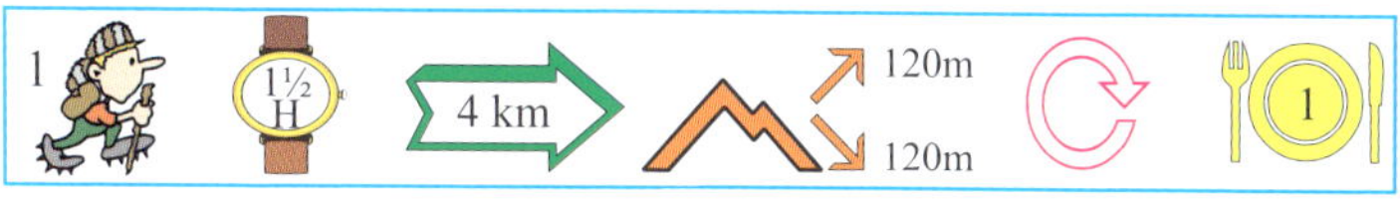

Access by car or taxi:
From **Camacha** follow the ER203 (Estrada Carreiras-Vale Paraiso) in the direction of **Poiso**. **Restaurante Abrigo do Pastor** is located approximately 3km from the **Camacha** junction on the right hand side of the road. Parking is available behind the restaurant.

We start the walk at the rear of the restaurant (Wp.1 0M) turning left into a cobbled lane a short distance from the car park (Wp.2 2M). Following the track, a narrow *levada* appears on our right as we descend to a rustic gate where the track ends.

Through the gate, signed 'Vereda do Pedreira', our route then becomes a narrow path with a number of paved stepped sections, leading us down beside the fast flowing channel, and here the vast expanse of the farming valley opens up in front of us.

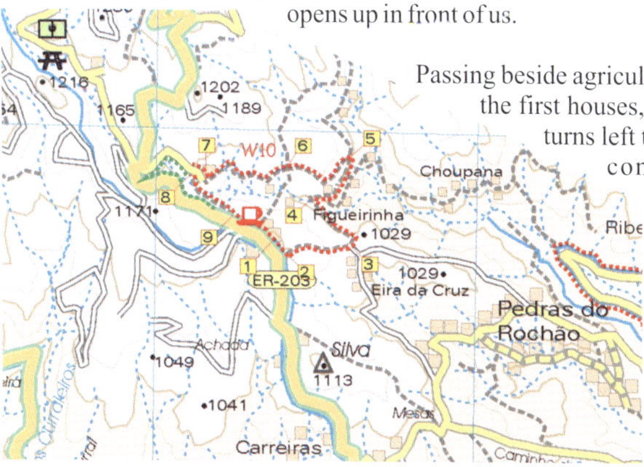

Passing beside agricultural plots and the first houses, the path soon turns left to meet a wide concrete track dropping deeper into the valley, eventually arriving at a junction with a vehicle track in the hamlet of

Figueirinha (Wp.3 22M). Turning left here, and left again after 30 metres, we head along a wide concrete track into the woodland and, contouring around the valley side, we eventually cross over a bridge where a pink house sits on the hillside to our right (Wp.4 27M).

With lovely views all around and our route adorned with patches of white chrysanthemums (in summer), the track becomes a two-wheel earthen track after the second house, ascending to the next derelict house when it narrows into a single file path, soon arriving at a junction with a forest track (Wp.5 42M). Going right would lead us to the island's waste disposal plant, which can be seen on the hillside across the valley, but here we go left, circling through the pine and eucalyptus forest until we reach a rustic fence and gate (Wp.6 56M).

... sheep roam freely ...

Passing through the gate, the track continues as it now makes a steady climb and soon the sound of the tinkling sheep bells heralds our arrival at a smallholding with sheep pens and farm buildings (Wp.7 70M).

Foxglove (Digitalis purpurea)

Throughout the year the sheep roam freely around and on each of our visits, large flocks have trundled across our path, plainly stirring recollections of life in Yorkshire for our border collie Lucy. We've walked this route at different times of the year and unlike most of the island, the contrast of seasons here is quite striking.

Holly

Deciduous species of beech, oak, willow and chestnut predominate and the landscape changes dramatically, with carpets of flowers below the fresh green leaves in spring and beautiful hues in autumn.

After the leaves have fallen, firs and pines take centre stage, hollies are laden with berries and there's often even a scattering of snow to complete the winter scene; all in all, a most picturesque location.

At the annual sheep-shearing festival

This area also hosts Madeira's annual sheep shearing festival; a charming event with a brass band, folk dancers and food and beverages stalls, the surrounding moorland thronging with local families enjoying this cultural spectacle and well worth a visit for anyone on the island around the first week of June.

From the farm buildings, the road becomes tarred as it climbs up through the rocky terrain and, after around 400 metres, arrives at a junction with the ER203 at **Montada do Pereiro**; one of the regional government's leisure and recreational facilities. This is an option for anyone wishing to extend the walk.

The forest track - final section to Abrigo do Pastor

Our main route leaves the tarred road a short distance beyond the farm, where a left hand track drops down to cross over a bridge (Wp.8 75M) before turning left again to climb up through the forest.

From here we follow the earthen track, which becomes stony underfoot, as it veers right and then left and, after running parallel with the ER203 for a short distance, meets the regional road just above **Abrigo do Pastor** (Wp.9 90M). This final section is only around half a kilometer, taking around fifteen minutes to walk, while the alternative route via **Montada do Pereiro** is around one and half kilometers, the last 800 metres being along the road.

Once back at the starting point, don't miss out on a visit to the restaurant and perhaps sample the *sandes leitão* (suckling pig sandwich), one of its specialities; you won't be disappointed. The food and ambience at this typical Portuguese establishment is excellent, reasonably priced and highly recommended.

11 LEVADA DO FURADO - RIBEIRO FRIO TO SANTO DA SERRA

Ribeiro Frio nestles below the high peaks within the largest area of natural forest on the island. The centre boasts many attractions including gift shops and restaurants as well as a trout farm and nature reserve and it's also the starting point for two of the official walking routes **PR10** to **Portela** and **PR11** to **Balcões**; see footnote for details.

This trail covers the first eight kilometres of **PR10 Levada do Furado** as far as **Lamaceiros** where we then head off on our final section to **Santo da Serra**. It's a fine challenging walk along one of Madeira's most well-trodden routes, passing through an exceptional area of *laurisilva*, a sub-tropical forest where spring and summer wild flowers flourish beneath the tree canopy, bringing colour and contrast. The second section passes through coniferous woodland with exquisite tree species. There are impressive rock cuttings and a wonderful series of tunnels and arches at **Cabeço Furado** - no torch required. New reconstruction along its whole length and with sturdy safety fencing erected on all necessary sections make this an almost vertigo-free route.

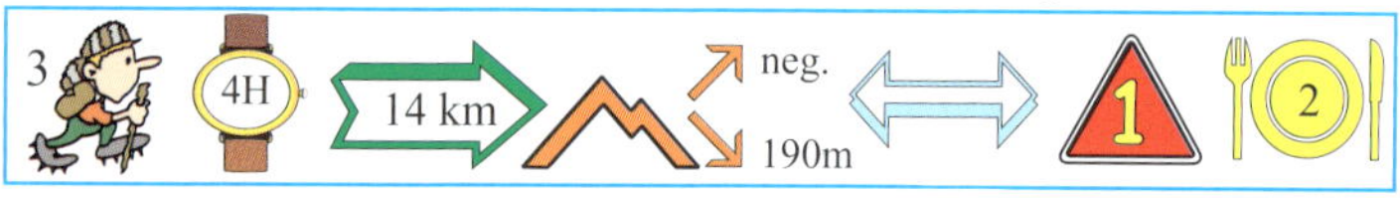

Access by hire car or taxi:
Take the ER103 to **Ribeiro Frio**. Drivers can park near the bars, lower down the road near the **Balcões** path, or at the picnic areas at the top end of the village.

Access by bus:
There is a limited daily service on route N°s 56, 103 and 138 between **Funchal**, **Ribeira Frio** and **Santana** & **São Jorge**. SAM bus N°20 and Interurban N°77 services run between **Funchal** and **Santo da Serr**a.

The sign at Wp.1

Starting at **Victor's Bar** (Wp.1 0M), a 'Portela' sign directs us down a paved pathway where we cross over a bridge and turn left, passing an information panel. Following the newly-laid path along the riverbank, **Levada Furado** soon appears on our right, the path then veering right to enter the forest.

A few minutes along, our path narrows but is protected with steel posts and wire; gaps in the vegetation allow views down to the north coast (Wp.2 10M). Passing through a rock cutting and over a water run-off at a small valley head, our trail arrives at a waterfall tumbling into the *levada* (Wp.3 23M). Our path continues through the forest, meandering around the hillsides, some sections wide and comfortable whilst others, though narrow and single file, are protected with sturdy fencing.

More views open up (Wp.4 33M) and along the whole route you'll find wonderful endemic species including orchids, geraniums, groundsel and moneywort. We soon arrive at the valley head of **Ribeiro do Bezerro** where new channels feed into the *levada* and sluice gates appear (Wp.5 52M). Our route turns left to cross the stream on a concrete bridge where many finches flit around, so tame and used to walkers, they'll take food from your hand.

Yellow Foxglove

Around fifteen minutes from the bridge, the *levada* passes alongside the rock face with dripping water and views across the tree canopy. We reach the first of a number of detours where steps lead down left to cross the stream rising again on the other side (Wp.6 67M). (Care must be taken here to spot the fencing line down the steps, as the channel shoulder suddenly becomes a ledge. Turn back immediately if you miss the fencing as the shoulder is unsafe from this point).

Passing through a rock cutting

At this first detour there is a small pool below the channel and, if visiting during July and August, look out for the rare Yellow Foxglove (Isoplexis sceptrum), an amazing endemic. Climbing steps, we pass through the first of a number of rock cuttings where the path squeezes through on paved sections (Wp.7 83M); another few minutes along a pretty shrine stands behind the channel (Wp.8 88M).

Lamaceiros water house

The *levada* runs into a tunnel, necessitating a detour on a lower path and a few minutes later, at a valley head, we leave the channel again on another detour. With more openings in the vegetation looking down on **Faial** and **São Roque**, the route turns sharp right to negotiate a huge and impressive rock cutting (Wp.9 106M). We arrive at a short side path on our left (Wp.10 139M) offering an excellent viewpoint on the edge of the promontory; a good place to take a short break before reaching an amazing section of the trail. At **Cabeço Furado** the *levada* clings to the valley side, passing along a section of narrow ledges through short tunnels.

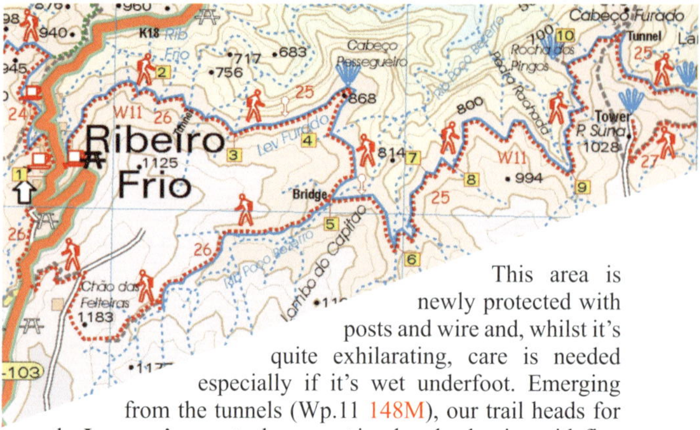

This area is newly protected with posts and wire and, whilst it's quite exhilarating, care is needed especially if it's wet underfoot. Emerging from the tunnels (Wp.11 148M), our trail heads for the **Lamaceiros** water house, set in a lovely clearing with fine oak trees (Wp.12 153M).

Passing in front of the building, our route turns right to reach a crossroads with a wide vehicle track and signposts. Left leads down to **Portela** and sharp right, up to **Pico do Suna** (See footnote for walking summaries for these options). Our route to **Santo da Serra** follows the wide woodland path straight ahead. Now following **Levada da Serra do Faial**, newly constructed until it reaches the **Santo da Serra** water house, the vegetation changes from natural forest to coniferous with magnificent specimens of Cedar, Juniper and Cypress along the route. In a few minutes the channel veers off right to round a small valley head; here a short detour leaves the *levada* to cross over the stream bed, reconnecting with the channel on the opposite side (Wp.13 162M). Following left, our route soon crosses over a forest track. A short distance ahead, the channel goes through a small tunnel with the path rising above it.

In fifteen more minutes there's another detour below the channel making a short descent into the woodland before ascending back to meet the *levada*. We arrive at the **Santo da Serra** water house (Wp.14 196M), a similar structure to the last one though with unique, amazing tree specimens beside the house.

Santo da Serra water house

Just beyond the building, a small track drops down left to reach a junction with the main forest track, our route to **Santo da Serra**. This can easily be missed, but by bearing right after the water house and continuing along the now disused *levada*, the channel crosses this main track and turning left here, the junction with the alternative route is found a few metres down the hill. Dropping down the forest track through mixed woodland where Mimosa and Maple dominate, the first house appears and the track becomes tarred. After a total of thirty minutes from the water house, we reach the ER102 on the outskirts of **Santo da Serra** (Wp.15 225M).

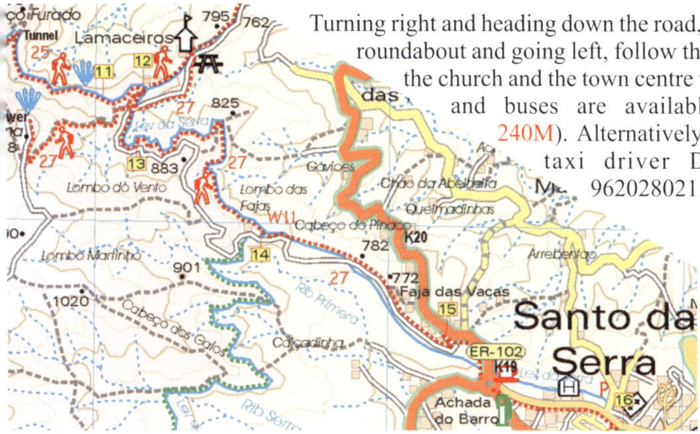

Turning right and heading down the road, we reach a roundabout and going left, follow the ER207 to the church and the town centre where taxis and buses are available (Wp.16 240M). Alternatively, call local taxi driver Duarte on 962028021.

Alternative:- Ribeiro Frio to Portela (3½ hours, 12 kms, descent 200m)

From the signpost at Wp.12, turn left following the earthen track, a couple of minutes later veering off left on a semi-stepped path alongside the **Levada da Portela**. At the bottom of the descent you arrive in the exotic gardens of the **Lamaceiros** forestry house with its magnificent cedars and tropical tree ferns.

Lamaceiros exotic gardens

Leaving the gardens and dropping drop down the road to a junction, the route goes off left, descending for around twenty minutes to reach a derelict water house. The *levada* divides so follow the left channel down a log-stepped descent. Entering an area of mature pines and eventually dropping down earthen steps, the trail comes to an end on the ER102. The **Portela** viewpoint is around 150 metres to the left.

Option to visit Pico do Suna (Ascent 180m, allow 1 hour for this extension)
From Wp.12 take the sharp right fork, signed 'Pico da Suna' and follow the broad grassy track as it winds up on a steep ascent through the tree-covered hillside. At a scissor crossing of tracks, the trail goes right to reach the impressive fire watch tower (1047 metres). This is a fantastic viewpoint to where the massif bulk of **Penha d'Águia** (Eagle Rock) towers over **São Roque** and **Porto da Cruz**.

PR11 - Vereda dos Balcões (Less than 1 hr - 3km return)
This trail follows a beautiful scenic route to one of Madeira's most spectacular *miradouro* viewpoints. It's a short walk with good pathways and no precipitous drops, so recommended for everyone. The best time to visit is during spring and summer when the flora is at its best and there's less chance of cloud invading the valley and blocking out the views.

12 SANTO DA SERRA - SERRADO DAS AMEIXIEIRAS - MADRE DE AGUA

Quinta da Serra exotic gardens

The green rolling hillsides and cooler climate of **Santo António da Serra** ensured it became a popular destination with the early English settlers, evidenced by a legacy of beautiful *quintas* around the village.

.. an avenue of camellias and azaleas ..

Quinta da Serra, just off the main square, is a fine example whose grounds are open to the public where you'll find magnificent trees and exotic plants, in particular an avenue of Camellias and Azaleas, so beautiful in early spring; deer, peacocks and waterfowl add to the charm of these gardens.

Another major attraction in the village and along the ER102 approach road is the Sunday market offering an assortment of local produce and crafts; it's extremely popular throughout the year and especially so at Christmas.

At the Christmas market

Our circular trail starts and ends close to the church and takes us along country lanes to the pretty hamlet of **Serrado das Ameixieiras**. Picking up a short section of **Levada dos Tornos**, we then visit the lovely chapel of **Capela Coração de Jesus** in **Sitio da Pereira** before dropping down an ancient pathway to return to **Ameixieiras**.

Indigenous species to look out for include fetid laurel, lily-of-the-valley, bilberry and heather, as well as the exotic flowering Himalayan ginger lily and banana maracuja, both making a splendid display throughout the summer.

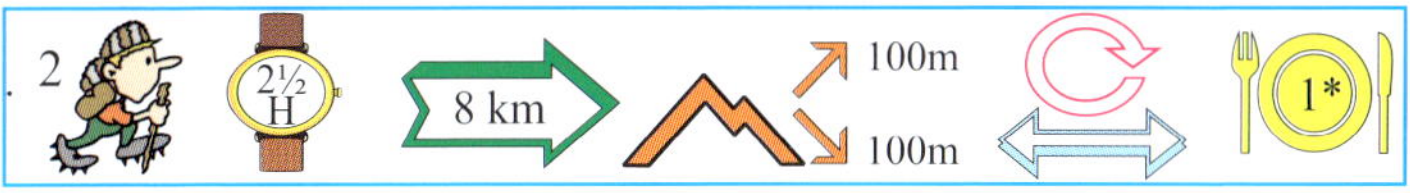

*** in Santo da Serra centre only**

Access by hire car or taxi:
Leave the VR1 at either Junction 15 to follow VE5 to **Camacha** then continue along the ER102 to **Santo da Serra** or, leave the VR1 at Junction 21 following ER207 to **Santo da Serra**. Park in the square beside the church.

Access by bus:
SAM Bus N° 20 and Interurban Bus N° 77 run services between **Funchal** and **Santo da Serra**.

We leave the village (Wp.1) along a narrow lane opposite the church and from here follow the walking notes from Wp.1 - 3 for Walk 13. Soon crossing over the bypass (Wp.2), we arrive 30 minutes later at a crossroads beside the boundary fencing of **Quinta Serrado das Ameixieiras** (Wp.3 30M).

Leaving Walk 13's trail at this point, our route descends left down a cobbled track, 50 metres ahead passing the main gates of the *quinta* and in another 100 metres, reaching steps coming down on our right and the lower *quinta* gates on our left. We will descend these steps on our return journey but for now we continue ahead.

Passing the first house on the right, a splendid old wine press appears also on the right and, just before reaching the next house, our route turns right down a narrow cobbled path descending through agricultural plots (Wp.4 35M)

The path drops down the side of the valley through pine woodland until it

reaches the **Levada dos Tornos** (Wp.5 40M); we turn right to follow it up stream. This is the final section of an extremely long *levada* flowing across to the east from below the **Funchal Ecological Park**; it was badly damaged in the Feb 2010 floods and whilst it's still in a bad state of repair, there are no problems with this route.

Himalayan or Kahili Ginger (Hedychium gardnerianum)

Passing beside two small barns on our left, we continue along a very pretty section of forest; after negotiating a bridge (Wp.6 45M) below a waterfall and weir (the bridge damaged but passable with care), we arrive at a derelict house on our right (Wp.7 50M).

Capela Coração de Jesus

Five minutes ahead we emerge onto the tarred surface of **Caminho Madre de Agua** (Wp.8 55M); leaving the *levada* we turn right to follow the lane up hill for around 400 metres to reach a school in **Sitio da Pereira** (Wp.9 70M).

Turning left here onto **Rua Mary Jane Wilson**, the chapel of **Capela Coração de Jesus** sits just below the road; during school hours it's possible to drop down the steps into the chapel gardens to view the lovely interior of the building.

Also known as **Capela de Nossa Senhora da Saúde** (Our lady of Health) and built in 1922, it was initially an orphanage for disadvantaged children, a legacy from the Franciscan charity founded by Mary Jane Wilson, a British Sister dedicated to the health, welfare and education of the ordinary people of the island.

Serrado das Ameixieiras

Leaving **Sitio da Pereira** behind and passing a few houses on either side of the road, our route continues for another 700 metres to reach an electricity tower and the ancient cobbled track on our right of **Caminho Serrado das Ameixieiras** (Wp.10 90M), our route back to the hamlet of **Ameixieiras**.

We drop down this track for around 25 metres before taking the first turn on the left. This is a narrow tarred driveway leading to two houses and a barn and after passing in front of the barn next to the agricultural plots we continue on a concrete path to reach the steps and *quinta* gate that we passed on our original descent into **Ameixieiras** (100M).

Our trail turns left here to return by the same route to the centre of **Santo da Serra** (Wp.1 150M), but it's really worth turning right to spend a little time in this hamlet first, the houses and gardens are so pretty and the local people appear most happy to see visitors.

13 SANTO DA SERRA to CAMACHA - LEVADA DA SERRA DO FAIAL

This popular walk follows a safe, vertigo-free and well-signed trail. Lying at 760 metres above sea level, the original route of **Levada da Serra do Faial** stretched 27 kilometres from the **Lamaceiros Waterhouse** in **Portela** to its end in **Choupana**, close to **Monte**. Unfortunately, much of the channel has now been obliterated by the creation of forest tracks and roads so it's no longer functional and its waters have been diverted. Nevertheless, it's a lovely walk where one can stride out and take in the pleasing and varied scenery.

The first and final sections of the trail are along country lanes and local roads; these are equally pleasant, passing through pretty woodland areas or through charming village settings.

Access by car or taxi:
Leave VR1 at either Junction 15 to follow VE5 to **Camacha** then continue along the ER102 to **Santo da Serra** or leave the VR1 at Junction 21 following ER207 to **Santo da Serra**. Park in the square beside the church.

Access by bus:
SAM bus N°20 and Interurban bus N°77 run between **Funchal** and **Santo da Serra**.

Santo da Serra church

We leave the village centre (Wp.1 0M) along the narrow lane of **Rua Padre João Pedro Gomes Henriques** opposite the church, following it for a short distance and, ignoring a right turn signed 'No Entry'; our route bears left along **Caminho da Pereira**. A few minutes later we cross the **Santo da Serra** bypass (Wp.2) and after a further 150 metres at a fork in the road, we bear right down the hill. Crossing a bridge over a stream, the stilt houses of **Quinta das Eiras** can be seen to our right.

Quinta Serrado das Ameixieiras

Our descent continues into the valley, crossing two more bridges before the lane starts to climb as we follow the boundary fence of **Quinta Serrado das Ameixieiras**, soon reaching a crossroads (Wp.3 30M). It's unfortunate that this charming old *quinta* can't be seen from the road, sitting in a fairy-tale setting deep in its wooded gardens. From the crossroads we turn sharp right and continue for 200 metres up the hill to a road junction, where we again turn right along **Rua Mary Jane Wilson** to arrive 600 metres ahead at the crossroads of **Sitio das Quatro Estradas** (Wp.4 40M) where the ER102 and ER 202 regional roads converge.

Taking the ER 202 **Poiso** road, we ascend again for another 600 metres, passing beside woodland to our left and the perimeter fencing of a pig farm to our right. At the end of the line of fencing we turn left onto a wide earthen track signed 'Camacha' (Wp.5 60M), the route of **Levada da Serra do Faial**, although the channel has been obliterated by the new earthen track. Following this path around the back of a maintenance depot, we soon veer off right into the acacia woodland; the golden mimosa particularly beautiful in spring. Six minutes along we see the ER102 snaking below us and a section of the old water channel also appears at this point.

Four minutes later we arrive at a gate across the track with pedestrian access around its side. There is now a deep valley on our left supporting huge conifers. The line of old oaks uniformly planted alongside the track are remnants of the original pathway, these trees adorning the *levada* along most of its former route. We soon arrive at a tunnel entrance (Wp.6 68M); no torch is needed as the tunnel is only around 10 metres long. A further two minutes then brings us to a wonderful waterfall. Dropping from around 50 metres above, it's wide and impressive after periods of heavy rain.

Our trail makes a slight incline before bearing right and soon another waterfall appears across the valley to our left. This is a lovely area with some magnificent conifers, the line of oaks continuing alongside the track. After crossing over a watercourse and passing a small cave on our right, we arrive at a disused water-house, dated 1942 (Wp.7 95M). Note the 'blue hat' on the building, obviously painted by some walking enthusiast; these symbols appear quite frequently on routes around the island.
Five minutes along brings us to a wide stone bridge where small waterfalls and pools can be seen to our right and left; along the track, we now pass beside an impressive water stairway on our right. This is a relatively new construction which provides water for the area of **Santa Cruz** on the south coast. Clearly the earthen track, which has now obliterated the *levada*, was excavated for this development. Just beyond the water stairway, another gate appears across the track (Wp.8 105M) so we walk around the side and continue along.

Crossing the forest track above Águas Mansas

With more scattered housing and the ER102 below us, we pass beside a fenced area of conifers before arriving at a T-junction with another forest track (Wp.9 120M) which leads up from the ER102 at **Águas Mansas** (meaning gentle waters) and continues to the water plant on the hillside above.

We continue straight ahead; in three minutes, after swinging right, we cross over a narrow water channel before arriving at a valley head where we cross over a stream on a stone bridge. A few minutes later we cross over a concrete road with street lights. As we approach the first houses, the track becomes concreted and as the number of properties increase, we arrive at a junction with the tarred road of **Azinhada do Ribeiro Serrão** (Wp.10 150M) where we turn right. Our route continues along the road, winding through a pretty wooded valley and past **Bar Rustico** approximately half way along (Wp.11 170M), a pleasant bar for taking a break.

Our route then continues around the valley to arrive at a T-Junction at **Rochão** (Wp.12 200M). Turning right, we cross the road diagonally before turning left where the *levada* is signed.

.. a cluster of old yellow-painted houses ..

We drop down the tarred lane, ignoring a concrete slope to our left and pass in front of **Bar Flõr Rochão** in the older area of **Rochão** where the *levada* channel is quite clear and even carries a little water. Soon crossing a stream bed, we pass in front of a cluster of old yellow-painted houses to arrive a few minutes later at a T-junction in **Igreja** (Wp.13 215M).

Now we turn left and drop steeply down before making a short ascent beside a water station on our right, then continue to descend to meet the old main road running through **Camacha**.

We're now standing in front of the town's Social Security Offices (Wp.14 230M).

We go right here to continue our descent - passing the old church **Antiga Igreja Paroquial da Camacha** on our right - before meeting the next junction around 200 metres ahead.

Turning left here, then immediately right, brings us into the main square (Wp.15 240M), a bustling centre with formal gardens, a lovely chapel and the famous basket making factory, showrooms and bar, all of which make it a favourite with tourists and walkers alike.

Capela de São José - Camacha Square

O Relogio wicker factory, Camacha

14 CAMACHA to MONTE

Following **Levada da Serra do Faial**, this wonderful walk passes through mixed woodland and dense pine forests as we head towards **Monte**. In the areas of deciduous woodland, you could be forgiven for thinking you are back in England; oak, beech, chestnut and pine abound as we pass beside old *quintas* along the *levada*.

The final section follows **Levada dos Tornos** passing through the **Choupana Hills Resort and Spa**. The route is relatively easy with no precipitous sections except on the approach to **Monte**, but this can be avoided by taking the lower path to cross the **Ribeira de João Gomes** valley before climbing up to the historic parish of **Monte**.

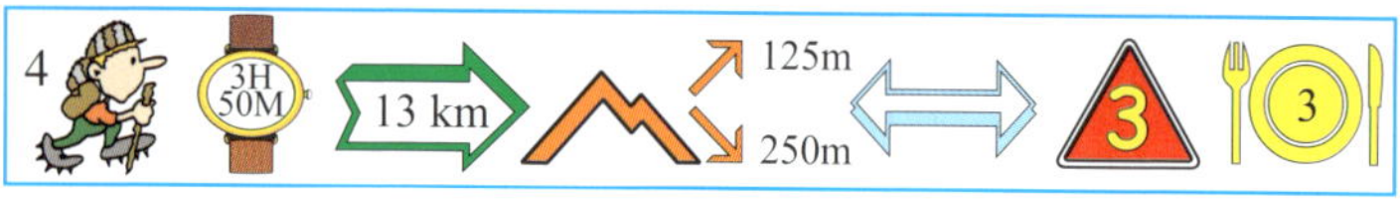

Access by car or taxi:
Leave VR1 at Junction 15 to follow VE5 to **Camacha**. At the roundabout, follow the signs for the centre. Parking is available in the main square.

Access by bus:
Horários bus N°129 runs between **Funchal** and **Camacha**. Return from **Monte** to **Funchal** on bus N°s 20,21 and 48.

Starting from the square in **Camacha**, (Wp.1 0M) we go right to follow **Rua Maria Ascensão**, signed 'Portela, Santo da Serra'. Heading up the road, we pass **Bar Boleo** on our right and the old church on our left before turning left 30 metres along by **Supermarcado Vila da Camacha**, signed 'Levada da Serra do Faial' (Wp. 2).

The old church, Camacha

Crossroads in Achadinha

The channel crosses under the road approximately 700 metres ahead and is signed in both directions (Wp.3 20M). We go left towards **Monte**, crossing a cobbled yard before meeting the channel just around the corner. Ten minutes' walk along the *levada* brings us to the quaint hamlet of **Achadinha**.

Just after the path becomes a narrow tarred road, the *levada* runs through a culvert and we find ourselves at a crossroads in the centre of the hamlet. Going straight ahead passing **Snack Bar Moises** on our right (Wp.4 32M), we rejoin the *levada* by climbing a short flight of steps beside the bus stop (Wp.5 35M). This whole section has the feel of a garden village and is a pleasure to walk through.

Maracuja banana adorns the woodland path

The wide woodland path alongside the *levada* is good underfoot and bordered with lovely flora; be sure to look out for the pink blooms of the Maracuja banana, which has colonized the trees along this section. A short distance along we cross over **Caminho da Madeira** (Wp.6 50M) and a few minutes later meet the huge concrete wall supporting the football ground above.

The next track we cross is the **Caminho Ribeiro Grande** and after contouring around a valley head, we arrive at the ER 203 **Camacha-Poiso** road (Wp.7 85M).

Entering an area with tall native evergreens, we enjoy views out to the **Desertas Islands** and soon pass the gates of **Quinta Ville do Paraiso**, next crossing a cobbled road to enter into more native woodland with laurels and tree heaths. Soon after crossing over a bridge at a valley head the *levada* has been tunnelled under a cobbled road. We follow the path to climb over the road and dip back down to the channel (Wp.8 100M). The vegetation begins to change as we pass through a mass of eucalyptus saplings, a little later reaching a ruined water-house on our right. From here onwards, the *levada* is completely disused and mostly covered over with ferns and other vegetation. A short distance from here we reach the end of the channel (Wp.9 130M) where we meet a cobbled track leading down to **Choupana Hills Resort**.

We turn left to descend the steep track and, after crossing over the ER 201 (Wp.10), continue to follow the sign for **Choupana Hills Resort**. Our descent continues to pass the gates of **Quinta da Choupana** and, a short distance ahead, **Quinta do Meio**, before arriving at a junction and bus terminus (Wp.11 144M); we go left, ignoring a sign pointing right for 'Choupana Hills'. Another 90 metres down the hill, the road crosses over **Levada dos Tornos** where we look for a gap in the wall on our right, to follow the channel upstream (Wp.12 145M).

Heading towards **Romeiros**, the *levada* passes through a green gate into the grounds of the **Choupana Hills Resort** (Wp.13 150M). After passing beside the chalets and taking in great views of **Funchal Harbour**, we exit through another gate at the western boundary. (It is essential to keep to the path anywhere inside the gated area.) We find ourselves in a lush green area of native forest with a very deep valley to our left; after crossing two streambeds where care is needed, particularly after heavy rain, we arrive at **Romeiros** (Wp.14 175M).

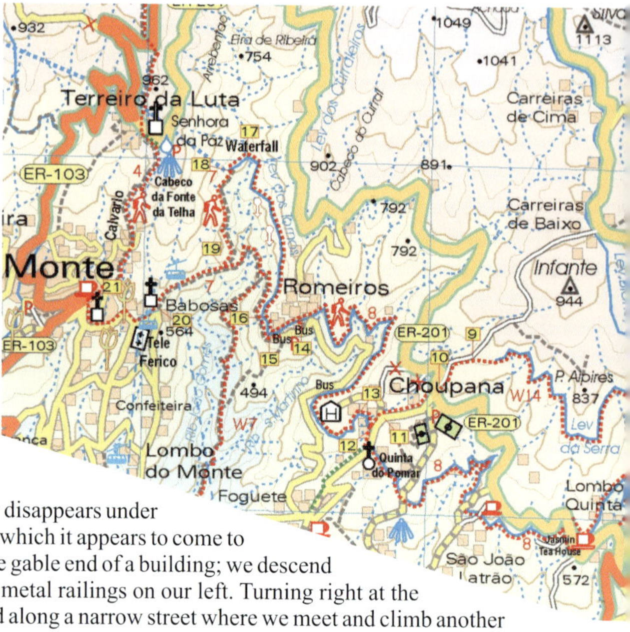

The *levada* now disappears under flagstones after which it appears to come to a dead-end at the gable end of a building; we descend a stairway with metal railings on our left. Turning right at the bottom, we head along a narrow street where we meet and climb another set of steps. After crossing over a road, we rejoin the channel (Wp.15 180M), covered over for a short distance until it leaves the village. Just after a right hand bend where we have dramatic views of **Monte** and **Funchal**, we find a narrow cobbled track descending sharply left from the *levada* (Wp.16 185M); here we have two choices.

Alternative Route (in poor weather and for vertigo sufferers)
Descend this path crossing a bridge over **Ribeira de João Gomes**, then climb up the other side to **Monte**, the best option in bad weather and for those subject to vertigo.

On the Levada dos Tornos path

Main Route (recommended for experienced walkers only)
We continue to follow **Levada dos Tornos**, though be aware that there are a number of very narrow and unprotected drops alongside the channel, so a head for heights and sure-footedness is absolutely essential.

Following the main route, we traverse around the valley. The channel, flanked by agapanthus, is good underfoot but soon becomes precipitous. After passing over a sluice gate, we reach a waterfall at the head of the valley and pass beneath this through a short tunnel where the *levada* is covered over (Wp.17 200M).

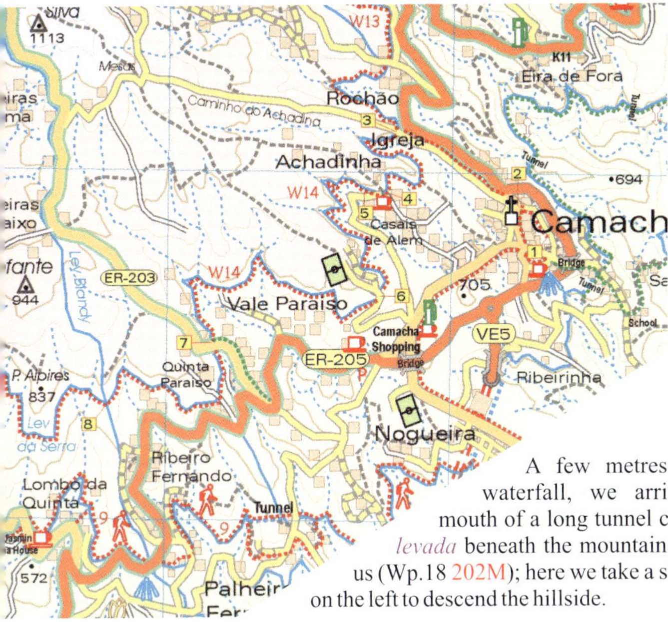

A few metres from the waterfall, we arrive at the mouth of a long tunnel carrying the *levada* beneath the mountain in front of us (Wp.18 202M); here we take a stony track* on the left to descend the hillside.

An impressive waterfall

***N.B.**
In our survey in May 2011, this pathway was found to be covered in debris from tree falls and landslips, but was passable with care.

At the bottom of the descent we meet a wide cobbled track on the apex of a bend (Wp.19 212M) signed right to 'Monte' and straight ahead along a narrower track, to 'Bom Sucesso'; this is the point where our two alternative options rejoin.

Taking the wide cobbled track, we continue up the hill to pass the cable car station for the *Teleférico* **do Jardim Botanico** and, a short distance ahead, arrive at **Babosas** square (Wp.20 220M), an area dominated by large plane trees. Continuing along **Caminho das Babosas**, we pass beside the **Funchal** cable car station, **Our Lady of Monte Church**, the famous toboggan run and the **Monte Palace Tropical Gardens**, to end our walk in the lovely **Largo do Fonte** (Wp.21 230M), where we can enjoy a well-deserved rest.

15 SANTANA - CALHAU - CAIS ANTIGO - SÃO JORGE

The coastal path from **Santana** to **São Jorge** must be one of the most wonderful routes on the island. There are stunning views of the coastline and mountains, beautiful flora, a shingle beach, ancient ruins, a spectacular old boat mooring and what's more, there's a natural lagoon plus a modern swimming pool complex and restaurant at the half way point.

The old church gateway

This route takes us down an ancient pathway from **Santana** into the historic settlement of **Calhau** where another cobbled path ascends into the parish of **São Jorge**. **Calhau** is a fascinating place with lots of history. For centuries it was the only port on the north coast, so it was an important trading centre. The ruins of a sugar cane mill and some warehouses remain as does the site of the church but this was destroyed by floods in 1660 and later rebuilt in **São Jorge**; now all that remains are stonewalls and the beautiful old church gateway looking out to sea.

Sea stocks on the approach to Cais Antigo

The settlement sits on a *fajã* and it's possible to make a one kilometre detour west to reach **Cais Antigo**, an ancient quay or jetty formed from the natural rocky promontory curving out to sea; this is **Ponta de São Jorge**. The path to the quay is cut into the rock around fifteen metres above the lapping sea; it's a sensational trail with amazing views and superb endemic flora. The end of the path leading onto the jetty has been destroyed and replaced with a makeshift wooden bridge used by local fishermen; however it has become dangerous so it's not advisable for walkers to go beyond the end of the path. Neither should any of this section be undertaken in bad weather.

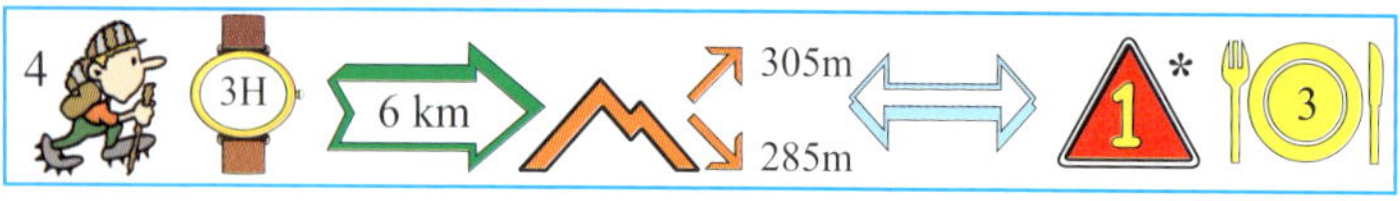

*** along cliff edge path to the old quay**

Access by car or taxi:

From **Funchal** follow the VR1 to **Machico** taking the VE1 to the **Santana** roundabout. Go straight ahead for 1.3km turning right along the road signed to 'Hotel Quinta do Furão'. Follow the signs for the restaurant and pub where parking is available.

Access by bus:
Bus N°103 provides a daily service from **Avenida do Mar** in **Funchal** leaving at 7.30am, returning from **São Jorge** at 16.48pm. There's also a regular bus service on route N°s 56 & 138 from **Funchal** to **Santana**, from where you can either walk (allow 15 minutes) or take a taxi to the starting point at **Hotel Quinta do Furão**.

Calhau from the cliff top path

From the car park (Wp.1 0M) a path heads up behind the **Quinta do Furão Restaurant**, leading to a cliff top walkway in the hotel gardens. The views from the gardens are spectacular, looking east across **Ilhéu da Rocha do Navio** as far as **São Lourenço** (Wp.2 5M).

Heading in a westerly direction our trail skirts the hotel boundary before narrowing as it leaves the grounds and continues along the cliff tops. The sea is aquamarine below us as superb views of the **Ruivo** mountain range appear on our left and our first view of **Calhau** appears in the distance ahead.

The path undulates as we make our way across the cliffs to reach a white house on the edge of the ridge. We take steps up the far side of the building to arrive at a tarred road and turning circle (Wp.3 20M). From this vantage point we enjoy fine views down into the **São Jorge** valley, with our onward route from **Calhau** to **São Jorge** visible as it snakes up the cliffs on the opposite hillside; the lighthouse at **Farrobo** is also in view from here.

We follow the road for a few minutes to reach a wide cobbled track going sharp right signed 'São Jorge - Calhau' (Wp.4 25M). The track, bordered with agricultural plots to our left, drops down behind houses; after passing between the final house and outbuilding, the path steepens and starts a zigzag down the

cliffs. The gradient is quite steep in parts but is good underfoot. The path veers away from the coastline to round a knoll, providing a little shade along the next section. As the vegetation opens around us, splendid views of the valley and mountains appear (Wp.5) before we descend further, our path now heading back towards the coastline.

The descent ends as we reach the **São Jorge** river, where a stone arched bridge leads us across to the ancient settlement (Wp.6 70M). A new path leads off the bridge down to the swimming pool complex and restaurant - on a hot day a cold drink and rest at this point is most welcome.

Our trail now continues close to the seashore and passing beside a few buildings on our left, we make a detour down a right hand path (Wp.7) to reach the ancient church gateway and the shingle beach. Returning to the cobbled track and heading to a house on the right with large palms in the garden, we reach a well on the left and a path ascending left (Wp.8 80M), this will be our route to **São Jorge**, though for now we continue along the main track on our detour to **Cais Antigo**.

We pass beside the ruins of the old sugar cane mill and other buildings before the path climbs a little and rounds the headland. The track is quite wide and cobbled along most of its length, but in places erosion has occurred and it becomes narrow and sandy, but with care and careful footwork, it's quite safe.

Chrysanthemum (Argyranthemum pinnatifidum)

The endemic flora along here is wonderful, with sea stocks, Madeira marigolds, the rare everlasting and chrysanthemum, just to mention a few.

On the approach to the old jetty we reach another left hand track (Wp.9 95M), an alternative route ascending the cliffs to reach a road leading to the lighthouse at **Farrobo**. However, we ignore this and 200 metres from the junction, reach the end of the trail where we find ourselves hemmed in by huge rock walls as we look across to the rudimentary bridge and the old mooring (see photo on next page).

From the quay we retrace our steps back towards the settlement and on reaching the well (Wp.8 110M), turn right to head up the first pathway to **São Jorge**.

The wooden bridge to Cais Antigo

Again, we are following a wide cobbled track which zigzags up the cliffs before passing into a side valley with much denser vegetation; from here we can look back on our descent route from **Santana**.

Looking back on our descent from Santana

It's a steady climb, following a *levada* upstream which occasionally meanders from side to side. Almost at the valley head, our route turns sharp right (Wp.10) to make its final ascent to a cobbled square where we find the remains of a primitive *fio* or cable lift, and a number of old buildings (Wp.11 155M).

Three roads converge here. The one immediately to our right leads to the top of the pathway ascending from **Cais Antigo** then continues on to the lighthouse, the second road on the right leads behind the village to a *miradouro* at **Vigia** before continuing on towards **Arco de São Jorge**. The road directly ahead is our route, which leads us past the cemetery and up to the church and village centre in **São Jorge**.

Ascending the road as it twists and turns, we arrive at the cemetery and the pretty little chapel of **Capela de São Pedro** before heading straight up the hill to reach the village centre and the lovely baroque church, **Igreja do São Jorge** (Wp.12 180M). This is the end of our walk, from where taxis and buses are available for the return route back to **Santana** or direct to **Funchal**; the bus stop is just a few yards away from the church.

16 SANTANA - FAJÃ DA ROCHA DO NAVIO

One of **Santana**'s best kept secrets, our trail leads to an ancient coastal settlement with a distinctive feel of bygone days. It's quiet, remote and until fairly recently was only accessible by an old path carved into the rock descending 365 metres to sea level. Once there you can walk along the *fajã* and across the pebbly beach to the small islet of **Ilhéu da Rocha do Navio**, situated a few metres from the shore which becomes cut off at high tide.

A weekend retreat

The fertile agricultural plots continue to bc tended; access is now made easier by the construction of a cable car (*teleférico*) operating at specific times during the week. Grapes, the dominant crop, are harvested at the beginning of September. The area is scattered with small agricultural barns and shelters as well as a few weekend retreats; the largest building is the nature reserve and education centre, its gardens devoted to the growth of endemic flora.

In 2001**Rocha do Navio Nature Reserve** became part of the Nature 2000 Network as a site of community interest and is now protected by Parque Natural da Madeira. Of particular interest is the potential habitat of Mediterranean monk seals, dolphins and marine and terrestrial birds as well rare endemic plant species found on the islets.

Our trail begins at **Santana** church, first dropping down a country lane to reach the *teleférico* station, then descending the ancient pathway and steps. The gradient is quite steep in places and some sections have been eroded, so care is needed, but there are no precipitous drops and protective fencing is in place where necessary. Our chosen return is by *teleférico* or you could retrace your steps (additional time 1 hour).

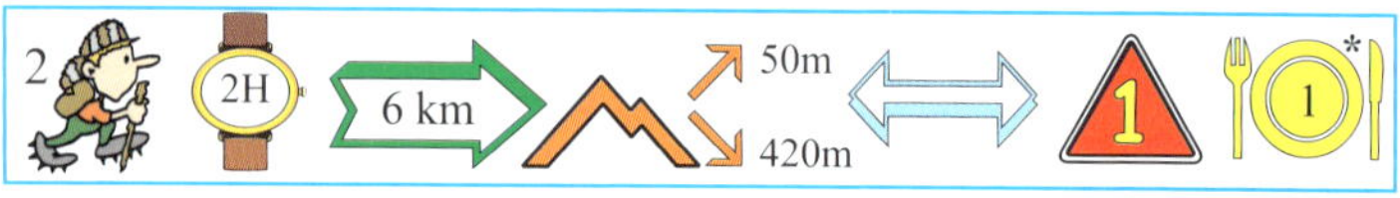

Access by car or taxi: *** in Santana centre**

From the south and east follow the VE1 to the **Santana** roundabout, turning left into the centre of the town. There is a car park on the right, across from the civic centre and the A-framed houses and gardens. The walk starts from the church situated close by in the town centre.

Access by bus:

There is a regular bus service (N°s 56, 103 & 138) from **Funchal** to **Santana** centre. The walk starts beside the church.

Starting on the left of the church (Wp.1 0M), we follow **Rua da Igreja**, a narrow rural lane heading in the direction of the coast. As we leave the houses behind we reach a junction with another lane on the right, signed 'Rocha da Navio Teleférico' (Wp.2 15M) which we take. The road makes a wide U-bend

The *teleférico*

before dropping further to reach a small car park above the cable car station (Wp.3 30M). A short steep track and steps lead down to the *teleférico* from where we enjoy our first stunning view of the coast with its high cliffs, the *fajã* and the islet a few metres out to sea.

.. steep steps ..

The path descends from the left of the platform, the trail dropping down on concrete steps beside the cliff and the dense vegetation. Five minutes along the steps zigzag; holding on to the sturdy wire and posts assists here. It can also be quite slippery in wet weather, so care is needed.

Prickly pear

Prickly pear, globularia and throatwort thrive here; at about eight minutes the path levels as it rounds a valley head, the deep gorge to our left dropping down to the sea. Descending again, we pass beside the first vines and reach a tiny farm building with a vine-covered tin roof.

Continuing down, waterfalls come into view as they crash from cliff tops to our right. The route becomes very craggy and the steps steep and uneven, before the path rounds a small clay promontory where the protective fencing has disappeared (Wp.4 60M). Almost down on the *fajã*, we arrive at a cave on our left housing an ancient wine press (Wp.5) and just below, we cross over a narrow *levada* with a branch heading down beside our path.

On reaching the first house and storage barns (Wp.6 70M), our route turns right passing vineyards and a well on our right.

.. storage barns ..

The flora throughout spring is so colourful, the whole place carpeted with nasturtiums plus sea stocks, marigolds and thistles.

We reach another junction; our route will go straight ahead, but first we go left to drop down to the Nature Reserve (Wp.7 75M), open only at specific times and usually by arrangement, though the small grounds are accessible. These are planted with endemic coastal plants including dragon trees, Echium nervosum, Mandon's chrysanthemum, butcher's broom and houseleeks.

The Nature Reserve

Returning to the junction, our path turns left, passing one or two small properties before we cross over a stream on a pretty hump-backed bridge (Wp.8 85M).

The pebbly shore is now to our left and pretty passageways and gateways to cottages and barns, appear on our right.

There are always one or two farmers or fishermen around ready to have a friendly chat; otherwise it's so quiet and peaceful and when the sun is shining and the sea is blue, it's paradise. At the end of the cultivated area we reach the cable car (Wp.9 90M) and from here make a five minute spectacular journey back to the station where we then retrace our steps to the starting point in **Santana** (Wp.1 120M).

.. passing passageways ..

Operating times for the Cable Car:

Saturday & Sunday
From 9.00am - 10.00am, 12.00 noon - 1.00pm, 6.00pm - 7.00pm
Wednesday
From 9.00am - 10.00am, 12.00 noon - 12.30pm, 6.00 pm - 7.00pm
Fridays
From 6.00pm - 7.00pm only

17 PORTO DA CRUZ CIRCULAR - LEVADA DO CASTELEJO

An old sugar cane mill

Porto da Cruz, hemmed in by **Penha d'Aguia** to the west and the stunning sea cliffs to the east, is one of the most charming towns on the island. Its architecture is a mixture of ancient and modern boasting a number of old sugar cane mills with their conspicuous chimneys.

Porto da Cruz promenade

There's the landmark hill with an old fortress on top and a fantastic coastal walk beside natural sea pools as well as a black sandy beach, a state of the art swimming area and a number of great bar restaurants beside the sea where you can enjoy a drink watching the world go by.

From the centre, our route climbs to the hamlet of **Cruz** to pick up **Levada do Castelejo** before circling the town at this elevated level. The trail passes beside a beautiful *quinta* on the edge of the forested slopes and drops down the ancient trail of the **Borracheiros** at **Cruz da Guarda** before making a final descent back to the town via an old municipal footpath.

There's an option to extend the route by following **Levada do Castelejo** west to its source in the beautiful **São Roque** valley. Those interested in walking this extension may prefer to take a taxi or bus to the *levada* (Wp.5), saving around one hour at the start of the walk.

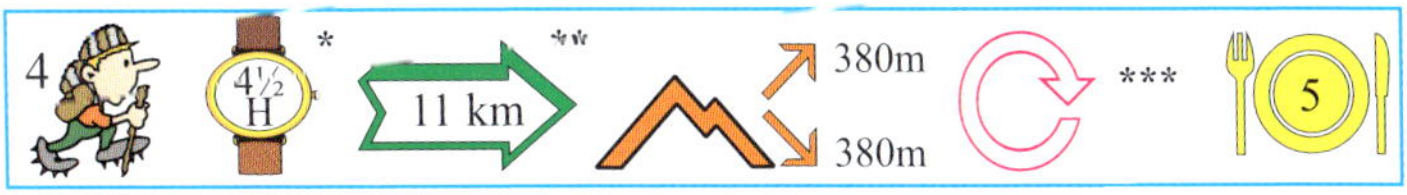

For the extension:

***add 2½ hours **add 8km ***vertigo risk 1**

Access by car or taxi:
Follow the VR1 to **Machico** taking the VE1 signed 'Santana' and 'Porto Cruz'. At the **Porto da Cruz** intersection follow the ER102 regional road into the centre of the village.

Access by bus:
Horario bus service Nº133 serves **Porto da Cruz** and **Santana**. For local services to **Cruz** village and **Referta**, check with the Tourist Information Office in **Machico** or **Funchal**.

The trail begins just below the church in front of the **Costa Linda Hotel** (Wp.1 0M), going straight ahead to pass through an arch under the *Centro Civico* building. Emerging onto the road, we turn left with the river on our right and continue along the main road to a zebra crossing. A narrow tarmac lane snakes up ahead slightly to the left; this is our route, the old road to **Cruz** village, narrow and steep but with little traffic to interfere with our pleasure. At around the halfway point, after crossing over the *expresso* slip road (Wp.2 30M), the track becomes cobbled.

On reaching the top of the lane the route turns left then left again next to **Katrepa's Bar** (Wp.3 45M), a popular refreshment stop with walkers and tourists. The narrow lane beside the bar ascends to a fork where **Levada do Castelejo** is signed in both directions (Wp.4 50M). The left fork reaches the *levada* in around five minutes, but our route takes the right fork along **Caminho da Terra Baptista**, heading up through the hamlet.

After passing a pretty chapel on our left, we reach the *levada* where it crosses over the road (Wp.5 60M). Here we have the option to extend the trail in a westerly direction to the source of the *levada* in the **São Roque** valley. (A summary of this route is given as a footnote).

On Levada do Castelejo

Our main circular route follows the channel east downstream; we pass beside agricultural plots and scattered houses with attractive gardens, the huge mass of **Eagle Rock** and the coastline dominating the views to our left.

After passing a filtration point at a valley head (Wp.6) we cross *caminho rural* to pick up the channel on the opposite side, signed 'Referta' (Wp.7 90M). This is where the shorter route joins from Wp.4. Our trail bends and twists around the valley heads and ten minutes after swinging around a pond (Wp.8 110M) reaches a tunnel under the road - no torch is needed.

The *levada* sweeps right against a high rock wall before reaching a valley head where a short detour crosses over a bridge (Wp.9 135M). Now passing through a pretty section of woodland, a second tunnel appears 10 minutes from the bridge. This is around 25m long with low headroom; again no torch is required.

The *levada* meets the ER102 (Porto Cruz/Portela regional road), where we leave the channel to cross over ascending **Caminho da Cruz de Guarda** also signed 'Quinta da Capela'. Our route heads into the hamlet of **Folhadal**, passing a viewpoint at the top of the hill, two minutes later reaching **Bar Marques** on our left, another good place to enjoy a drink. Around two hundred metres beyond the bar a sign appears on the left 'Caminho Municipal (Folhadal - Serrado)' (Wp.10 150M).

Quinta da Capela

This is our return route back to **Porto da Cruz** and is an option for shortening the walk by missing out the next section. However, our favoured route continues ahead, returning to this point in just over one hour's time.

Another few hundred metres along there's another signpost where steps lead up to **Quinta da Capela**, a beautiful 17th century manor house (now a hotel) surrounded by exotic gardens sitting on top of the hillside overlooking the coast. It can't be seen from this position although there are good views from a little further along.

Ignoring another stairway on the right and continuing to where the road crosses a stream bed and swings sharp left, we turn right up concrete steps with an ochre coloured wall on the left of the stairway (Wp.11 160M). The steps zigzag up quite steeply, the beautiful **Quinta da Capela** now in view.

Almost at the top of the steps, opposite an A-framed barn with a tin roof, we ignore a left turn to a house, instead going straight ahead to the end of the stairway (Wp.12 170M) meeting a muddy path with a narrow *levada* running alongside.

Following the channel the path levels contouring around a high banking, then two minutes later passes below a concrete water tank, we climb up the left of the tank on muddy steps to continue following the *levada*. The channel comes to an abrupt end at a valley head (Wp.13 180M), the path crossing over the rocky riverbed to pick up an old channel on the opposite side. At the time of our survey, a couple of small landslides had obscured this old channel, but a few metres ahead the line is clearly seen.

The next short section needs careful concentration as the route becomes quite vague. The channel turns right and fifty metres later after passing beside a small orchard on our left, it splits into two. So keeping our eyes to the ground we look out for a very narrow left hand branch - around nine minutes from the river. Following this left branch down grassy steps and slope, a pylon appears on our right. (If you miss this small junction, you will find yourselves scrambling under dense vegetation, so turn around immediately to find the correct route).

Continuing to descend for another few minutes, the path rounds a small valley head crossing over a stream on a concrete slab. The path narrows becoming rather slippery underfoot. It takes another few minutes to reach scattered houses and terraces. Ignoring steps leading down to buildings on our left, we continue ahead to emerge onto a steep tarmac lane. Now in **Cruz da Guarda** we're following **Caminho da Ladeira**, an ancient pathway linking **Porto Cruz** to **Portela**, the trail of the *Borracheiros* who used this route to trade their wine in the higher settlements.

Turning left and dropping down the lane, we arrive at a junction with a wider road (Wp.14 200M), our route back to Folhadal. Going left at this junction, it's just under one kilometre, passing the steps we ascended earlier, to return to 'Caminho Municipal (Folhadal - Serrado)' (Wp.10 215M), our onward route back to **Porto da Cruz**.

Turning right onto **Caminho Municipal**, the trail descends the concrete driveway dropping beside the houses. At the last house the drive turns sharp left then ends, the path now becoming a mixture of cobbles and clay making a U-turn down into the valley - it's quite slippery in places so a walking pole is useful here.

We pass through a disused agricultural area evidenced by the appearance of taro root, sugar cane, bananas and giant reeds but it's a lovely spot with views of the surrounding mountains all around us as our pathway descends towards the river.

The pretty stream and hump backed bridge

Five minutes from the start, we pass beside a waterfall crossing over a pretty hump backed bridge; the path is wide, with mimosa blossoms, wild flowers and tethered goats adding to the scene.

A few minutes ahead, the first views of **Serrado** appear (Wp.15), the route crossing high above the tunnels on the VE1 Expresso before arriving at a T-junction with the ER102 (Wp.16 230M).

We turn right, following the road for just one minute before turning right again onto **Caminho Padre Caetano Soares** (Wp.17 231M), once the original route of the municipal pathway across the **Serrado** ridge, but the village road has now obliterated it.

Eagle Rock (Penha d'Aguia)

One minute ahead, we pass a snack bar and soon are treated to amazing views of **Penha d'Aguia** and **Vila Porto da Cruz** that appear on our left; the coast is ahead of us and the village of **Larano** stands on the mountainside to the east.

The town from Serrado Ridge

We pass beside a number of pretty houses and gardens before the road starts to ascend to **Cabeço**, later descending the western side of the ridge. The road then comes abruptly to an end at a builder's gate (Survey Feb 2011), beyond which is the large excavation project on the **Serrado** escarpment.

There's a short pedestrian access to the left of the gate (Wp.18 255M), then immediately turning sharp left, we follow a cobbled stairway descending steeply towards the town: this is the final section of **Caminho Municipal**.

Passing a rocky gorge on our left, the path comes to an end at a tarred road (Wp.19 260M) which comes over a bridge off the ER102. We're now in front of a yellow public building **Flores de Maio - Associação Cultural**.

Turning left then immediately right, the route makes a final descent into the town arriving at a junction with a cobbled road leading off right (Wp.20 265M) and a cobbled bridge straight ahead. Our route is right to the promenade, but it's worth crossing over the bridge to see the prettiest cemetery on the island as well as the lovely church square.

Back at the junction we descend to the promenade turning left to reach the sea view bar restaurant of the **Costa Linda Hotel**. From here we continue a few metres up the cobbled lane beside the hotel to return to our starting point (Wp.1 270M).

Extension along Levada do Castelejo (Add 2hrs 30mins - 8kms)
This extension leads us through mountainous landscape adorned with lush vegetation before transcending into the *laurisilva* and ending at the source of the *levada* beside picturesque pools and waterfalls at the **São Roque** riverbed. It's a relatively easy walk although you need to be sure-footed and have a head for heights as there are one or two precipitous sections along the route.

18 LEVADA DO CANIÇAL - MAROÇOS to RIBEIRA SECA

Levada do Caniçal is a classic *levada* route in the east of the island combining easy walking with impressive flora. It's popular, so expect to meet lots of walkers throughout the day. We head into rural communities and across cultivated terraces as well as through deep valleys, ravines and areas of natural forest, enjoying lovely views all the way.

.. a popular route ..

Access by car or taxi:
Follow the VR1 to **Machico** taking the VE1 towards **Porto da Cruz**. At the end of the third tunnel turn right, signed 'Maroços' and 'Portela', then turn right at the junction after the bridge. The *levada* is signed on the left around 25 metres from the junction across from **Bar A Calçadinha**.

Access by bus:
S.A.M. Bus N°156 serves **Maroços**. N°s 23 and 113 run between **Machico** and **Funchal**, the latter also continuing to **Caniçal** via **Ribeira Seca**.

Beginning at **Bar A Calçadinha** (Wp.1 0M) we pick up the channel on a paved section, crossing a tarred road a couple of minutes later to meet the open channel. Strolling between random houses and agricultural terraces, our trail heads in and out of small valleys, mountain slopes rising on our left and deep valleys often appearing on our right.

Houses cling to the steep slopes

After crossing a tarred road (Wp.2 10M), the route swings into a valley. We cross the head on stepping-stones alongside a weir (Wp.3 15M) before heading back out in a southerly direction. Houses in various styles cling to the steep slopes; five minutes from the weir, we reach the main village, albeit at an elevation high above the centre. Here, the *levada* crosses over a narrow stairway dropping between the houses, the final section of the **PR5 Vereda das Funduras** leading down from **Portela**. The local people are extremely friendly and happy to stop for a chat with the many walkers who pass this way.

Stopping for a chat

Rural houses border the *levada* (Wp.4 25M) and protective fencing appears on steep sections before we head into another valley, the forested areas now appearing much denser.

We cross a bridge over the **Ribeira das Cales** (Wp.5 59M) and a few minutes ahead find a *fio* on the channel shoulder (an old cable used for agriculture and *levada* maintenance) (Wp.6 64M). A short distance ahead we enter a fifteen metre tunnel (Wp.7 84M) (no torch required). A few minutes after emerging we take in stunning views over **Machico** and the motorway network sprawling across the landscape.

Into the short tunnel

After passing beside a rock face with dripping water (Wp.8 104M) the vegetation becomes more natural as we leave habitation behind and head into another valley. Slopes rise on our left and we make a detour down a few steps to cross the stream on stones (Wp.9), picking up the channel again on the other side. The valley is beautiful here with agricultural huts dotted across the landscape.

Leaving this behind, we reach a stone well on our right and rounding the next bend, are amazed to find a bar (Wp.10 126M) which on first sight appears to be in the middle of nowhere, nevertheless a very welcome sight and buzzing

.. a cute little tin hut ..

with happy faced walkers, all equally relieved to have stumbled upon **Bar O Jacare**, a new enterprise converted from an old warehouse in the **Noiá** valley. Our route now swings left into the charming **Ribeira Seca** valley (Wp.11). After passing beside pretty houses and gardens, the valley deepens and become craggy and remote, the hills of **Boca do Risco** now rising above us. We cross a stream, the scene enhanced by a cute little tin hut surrounded by exotic flora. The largest species is Heliconia bihai, a red ornamental plant related to musa, the banana plant (Wp.12 156M).

The ancient trail to Boca do Risco

Ten minutes later we arrive at an old signpost at a junction with a diagonal path crossing the *levada* (Wp.13 166M). We are now on **Vereda da Boca do Risco** the ancient, yet renowned and dangerous trail connecting **Caniçal** with **Porto da Cruz**. At this point we have two options; to leave the *levada* following **Vereda da Boca do Risco** down into **Ribeira Seca** (our choice), or to continue on the *levada* for a further 45 minutes to reach the **Caniçal Tunnel** on the ER109 which provides the opportunity to extend the route as far as **Caniçal** or to **Pico do Faço** or **Machico**.

We leave the channel and head down into the village of **Ribeira Seca**. The narrow, stony path descends between agricultural terraces and houses. Ignoring all steps and paths leading off to the right, we continue to descend until we reach the end of the path just above the village street. A few steps now lead us down to **Bar Boca do Risco** in the village centre (Wp.14 180M).

Again, you'll find the villagers here extremely friendly and helpful and there's a bus service from the bar into **Machico**. Alternatively you can either walk down to **Machico** (allow around 45 minutes) or call the local taxi driver Fernando (917 840 983) who will take you back to your starting point in **Maroços** (Taxi fare around €7).

PR5 Vereda das Funduras (3hrs 30mins, 8.7 km)
Beginning at the **Portela** viewpoint overlooking **Porto da Cruz** and **Penha d'Aguia**, this wonderful forest walk passes through the best area of *laurisilva* on the south side of the island before reaching **Funduras** and eventually the village of **Maroços**. (See Walk! Madeira for full walking notes on this route.)

19 SÃO LOURENÇO - PRAINHA - PICO DA PIEDADE

Breathtaking scenery, wild landscapes, amazing rock formations - **São Lourenço** is unique. Unlike most of the island, it's quite arid, providing a habitat for a number of rare endemic plants. Around the peninsula, dragon trees (Dracaena draco), once native to the area, have also been planted alongside exotic Agava attenuata and red sword aloe.

This trail, an alternative to the well-known (**PR8**) route across the peninsula may be short, but it's equally stunning and offers a number of options for a memorable day out. Climbing firstly to the ancient chapel on **Pico da Piedade**, the route then drops down to the **Prainha**, the island's only natural sandy beach, for a few hours swimming or sunbathing. There's also a beach bar open throughout the summer period and at weekends.

Close by is **Quinta do Lorde**, the impressive holiday resort recently created around the **Caniçal** marina. Its popular **Captain's Bar** is open daily.

* summer and weekends

Access by car or taxi:
Take the VR1 to the **Caniçal** roundabout following the signs for **Prainha** and **São Lourenço**. Roadside parking is available at **Prainha**.

Access by bus:
SAM Bus N°113 provides a frequent daily service from **Funchal** to the peninsula via **Machico** and **Caniçal**.

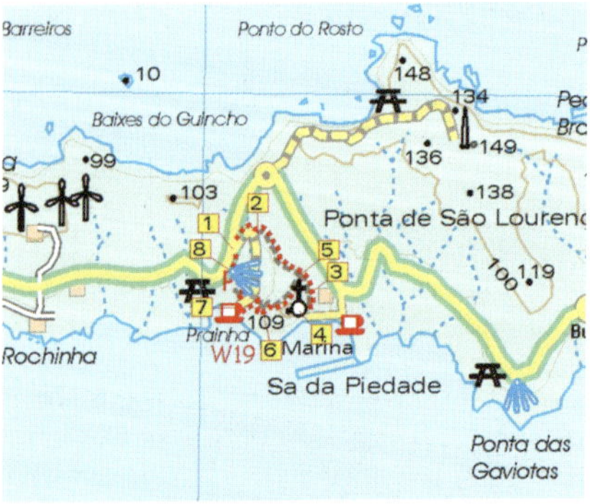

We start the walk a few metres east of the **Prainha** lay-by (Wp.1 0M) where a gate abuts a paved driveway leading down into the valley below. After a sharp U-bend the driveway continues down to the beach, but just beyond the bend we take a narrow path off left (Wp.2 5M) and a few metres ahead, after passing the first dragon tree, turn right, climbing slightly to reach six old stone bollards. Fifteen metres ahead, a narrow path drops down on our right - we return to this point for our final descent to the beach, but for now we continue ahead for a few metres to reach a broad earthen track.

Quinta do Lorde and the marina

Our route turns right, following the track for a short distance to reach a cobbled stairway on the right (Wp.3 15M), our route to the chapel. As we climb, both north and south coastlines come into view, the eastern lowlands stretch out around us and **Quinta do Lorde** and the marina are down to our left.

Capela Nossa Senhorsa de Piedade

The steps make an easy zigzag up the hillside, soon arriving on the summit beside the **Capela Nossa Senhora de Piedade** (Wp.4 20M), location for the annual festival of Our Lady of Mercy (Nossa Senhora da Piedade), patron saint of fishermen. Each year on the third weekend of September, a procession leaves **Caniçal** in a flotilla of decorated boats on its route to **Quinta do Lorde**, the pilgrimage then continuing on foot up to the chapel.

Leaving this stunning viewpoint, we retrace our steps down to the track and head back towards the stone bollards, but now around fifteen metres before reaching the bollards, our route turns off left towards the beach (Wp.5).

Red sword aloes on the approach to the beach

Crossing over the grassy hillside heading towards the beach, the narrow path becomes a little vague in places but soon arrives in front of a large rock below the cliffs. Going right and descending towards the dragon trees and red aloes, the trail emerges onto a wide path and gully.

Around the next bend the gully turns off left (Wp.6), our route continuing along the line of exotic aloes before rejoining the paved driveway to reach the beach bar (Wp.7 40M). Steps lead down to the sandy cove hemmed in by the large sea cliffs; it's idyllic, particularly during the quieter winter season. After a swim or a spell of sunbathing it's time to tear ourselves away and head back. Now ignoring the paved track, we take the left hand concrete drive behind the bar to reach steps ascending on the left.

This paved stairway zigzags steadily up the hillside leading us back to the starting point (Wp.8 55M); there are now two additional options. It's around 500 metres east along the road to the driveway of **Quinta do Lorde** or an additional 500 metres to the start of the **Ponta do São Lourenço** trail across the peninsula; it's a question of available time and energy - both are worthy of a visit.

PR8 - Vereda da Ponta de São Lourenço (8 kms, 2½ hours return)
Beginning at **Baia d'Abra**, this well-trodden route follows an old mule track across the peninsula, passing along a natural land bridge before arriving at **Casa do Sardinha**. The viewpoints from the north and southern cliff tops are breathtaking; try to visit on a clear day when the route is enhanced by the sparkling blue sea and sky.

Resort Quinta do Lorde
Set in a beautiful bay beside the marina, this new coastal village has been built in an architectural style sympathetic with the area and its surroundings.

Quinta do Lorde restaurant

Spreading up from the coastline and marina, the complex is hemmed in by the surrounding cliffs and hillside and when completed will comprise a hotel, apartments, restaurants, swimming areas, leisure facilities, a market and a church.

20 CALHETA SLOPES - LEVADA DA ROCHA VERMELHA - LEVADA NOVA - CALHETA

Over the last few years, the picnic site on the ER211 has become a popular collection and drop-off point for organized walking companies. Having recognized the benefits of the **Calheta** tunnel, they now use it daily to lead groups to and from **Rabaçal**. So whatever time of year you visit, you're likely to meet crocodiles of people setting off from this point on the routes to **Risco** and **25 Fontes**.

Strange then, that none seem to take this alternative route down the **Calheta** slopes to **Levada da Rocha Vermelha** and beyond. It's a lovely trail with an easy descent and we can have it all to ourselves to enjoy the peace and quiet amongst the birds and flowers.

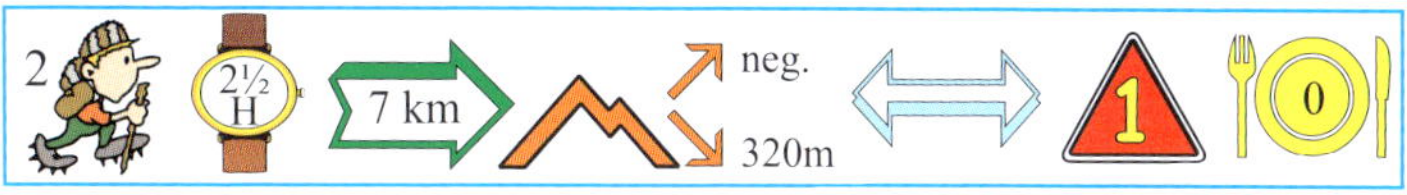

Access by car or taxi:
Leave the ER222 in the centre of **Estrela da Calheta** following the ER211 for 5 km to reach the picnic site in **Lombo do Salão**. Alternatively approach from the ER105 **Paúl da Serra** road dropping down the ER211. Parking is available beside the shelter.

The water-house at Wp.2

Just above the picnic site (Wp.1 0M), we take a broad track heading into the forest signed '25 Fontes and Risco'.

Contouring around the valley side and crossing a cattle grid, we arrive at the pretty water-house at the head of the **Calheta** valley (Wp.2 15M). The routes to **Rabaçal** leave on the left of the house, going north into the tunnel, but looking south we can see our trail winding down the hillside with **Levada da Rocha Vermelha** at the bottom of the descent.

Calla Lily

The cobbled pathway leaves directly in front of the water-house and descends in easy loops on its way down the slopes. Eucalyptus and pines surround us on the valley side and our route is hedged with bracken and brambles. As we drop deeper into the valley, mimosa trees appear all around and depending on the time of year, clumps of both Calla and Belladonna Lily give lovely displays.

We pass through a rustic gate and then drop down a few rocky steps to arrive at the riverbed and *levada* (Wp.3 35M).

Belladonna Lily

The tunnel

Levada da Rocha Vermelha is an extremely pretty and well-maintained channel which flows through the mountain from the **Ribeira da Janela** valley via a tunnel, visible on our left. Crossing over the river, it's clear that the channel is fed at this point from the river before it continues on to the hydropower station.

Following the channel south with a deep gorge on our right, we soon arrive at a water divider where a huge pipe crosses the *levada* taking water to the hydropower station (Wp.4 45M). We cross this section on a weir within the walled tank, safer than walking along the outer wall.

Looking right along the next section, **Levada Nova** is visible at the lower level, which we'll pass along later. Approaching the next water house, we find

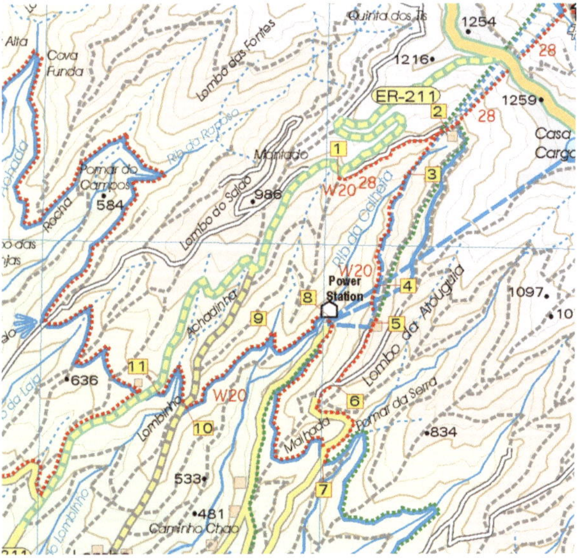

Crossing the Ribeira da Calheta

a paving stone over the channel where a path comes down from the left. This also originates at the head of the valley just beyond the one we've descended, thus offering an alternative route to make a circular back to the starting point. Meanwhile, our main route continues to the water house at the end of **Levada da Rocha Vermelha** (Wp.5 55M).

Leaving the house, we continue down the access road, soon meeting a forest track coming down from the left (Wp.6 61M); here our track bends to the right and we continue to drop down to another junction. There are good views over **Loreto** and **Calheta** and at this point, the road becomes cobbled.

We descend a little further and veer right passing beside a pretty restored cottage. A little further along the track crosses over **Levada Nova** (Wp.7 84M) and we go right along the channel as it passes through the forest. There's an abundance of agapanthus along this stretch and some sections of narrow shoulder, so care is needed. We reach a cobbled lane leading from the hydropower station where the *levada* crosses under the lane and continues to circle in front of the building - note there's no pedestrian access along this section, so instead we turn right and head up to the building, passing across a veranda at the front and then over a bridge behind. To our right the **Ribeira da Calheta** falls into a reservoir which then feeds into the station, the excess falling over a race and feeding the *levada*. Turning left after the bridge, we reach a flight of steps (Wp.8 110M) to descend and rejoin the channel.

Along our final section of the *levada*, the water flows in a deep concrete channel standing over a metre high, the water extremely clean and fast flowing. We cross a bridge over a small gorge (Wp.9 121M) with views over **Lombo da Atouguia**, **Calheta**, wonderful in late spring when the profusion of broom is in flower.

Just after passing some beehives on our right, the *levada* goes under a cobbled road (Wp.10 141M); we climb steps and descend again on the other side and a few minutes later reach the end of the walk on the ER211 (Wp.11 148M).

We've a number of options from this point; we can follow the road right for 2km with a 300m ascent to return to the picnic site, go left descending into **Estrela da Calheta** where buses and taxis are available (3km with a 350m descent) or could call a taxi to collect us at this point.

21 RABAÇAL - RISCO WATERFALL & 25 FONTES

The valley of **Rabaçal** on the western slopes of the **Paúl da Serra** plateau is one of the most beautiful locations on the island so unsurprisingly, one much frequented by walkers. The busy car park alongside the ER110 is the starting point for eight trails; whenever you visit, you're likely to find it bustling with tourists and hikers. From here the view towards the **Rabaçal Forestry Post** (**Posto Florestal do Rabaçal**) nestling 220 metres below is breathtaking; the deep-forested valley below is our destination on this wonderful trail combining the two official **PR6** and **PR6.1** walking routes.

There are some very narrow and precipitous sections along the **Levada das 25 Fontes** and whilst these are well protected with steel posts and fencing, the Forestry Service issues a warning that the **PR6** can cause vertigo and that people should not lean on or put weight on the protective barriers. That said and understood, this is a superb and well-trodden route to a wonderful location which will not pose problems for the majority of people.

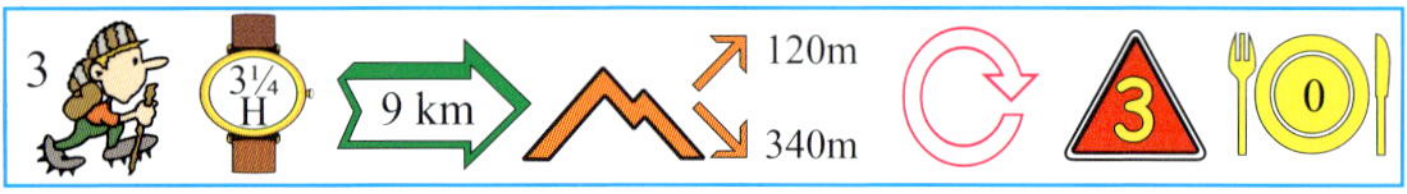

Access by car or taxi:
The viewpoint lies at 1290 metres above sea level and is situated on the ER105 approximately 4.5 km west of the **Paúl da Serra** crossroads. From the car park we have the option to walk down the tarred access road (1.8 km taking around 25 minutes) or to take the shuttle bus, which operates daily (except Christmas Day), from 9.30 a.m. until 6.00 p.m. at approximately 20 minute intervals.

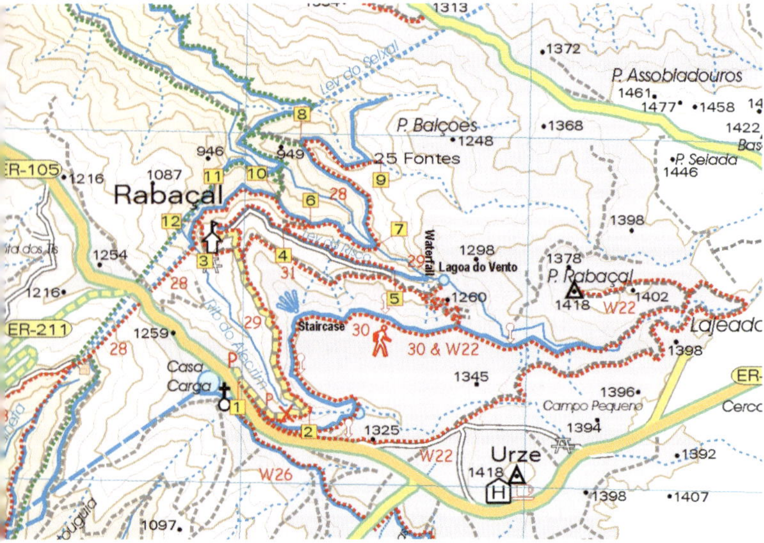

Starting at the car park (Wp.1 0M), we follow the access road as it bends and twists on its descent to the forestry house. At a left hand bend we pass a pretty pond on our right where the road crosses over **Ribeira do Alecrim** (Wp.2 10M), then continue down through the heath forests to the shuttle bus terminus close to the house (Wp.3 25M). Fingerposts direct us right along a paved path through shady woodland, before we meet a junction with a track coming in from the left, an alternative route from the forestry house. The **Levada do Risco** now flows on our right and we follow it for a short distance.

Sonchus (Shrubby Sow Thistle)

At another set of fingerposts (Wp.4 35M) our route goes straight ahead signed 'Risco', though we'll return to this point for the next section of the trail to **25 Fontes**. From the signpost it's less than a kilometer to the waterfall. As we go deep into the forest, many wonderful endemic plants can be spotted; Madeira Orchids, Anemone-Leaved Cranes-Bill, Madeira Moneywort and Shrubby Sow Thistle, the latter resembling giant dandelions, all thrive.

Risco Waterfall

Twenty minutes after the sign we arrive in the semi-circular basin of **Risco Waterfall** from which viewpoint we can admire this spectacular natural landmark (Wp.5 55M). The waterfall crashes down the volcanic rock face, disappearing from view into the valley below. From this point the *levada* shoulder is no longer passable but can be seen as it tunnels into the rock, leading behind the waterfall and then on through further tunnels around the wooded rock face. In winter following heavy rain, the waterfall - impressive at any time - is quite spectacular.

The Levada das 25 Fontes

The pathway along the whole route is protected with rustic fencing on exposed sections with steel posts and fencing added on the approach to the waterfall viewpoint.

After absorbing the beautiful views, we return to the path division and go right, descending the stone-laid path as it drops steadily through the forested valley to bring us to a T-junction beside the **Levada das 25 Fontes** (Wp.6 90M).

Turning right, the trail follows the channel upstream, five minutes later crossing the deep gorge of **Ribeira Grande** (Wp.7 95M). We meet a series of steps where we leave the channel for a short distance, before ascending more steps to pick it up again at a small water station. From here our route becomes precipitous in places, but the pathway is well protected and there's lots of vegetation to make us feel secure. A number of sections of pathway is single file, so we need to be prepared for the long crocodiles of walking parties passing in both directions which can often delay progress.

At this lower altitude the vegetation has changed with *laurisilva* taking over from the heath forests higher up the valley. It's dark and lush, ideal for many more indigenous plants and it's also a lovely stretch for views down the **Ribeira da Janela** valley. Shortly we arrive at a path descending on our left (Wp.8 115M), one of the routes down to **Levada da Rocha Vermelha** and an even longer trail along **Levada da Ribeira da Janela**, which ends in **Lamaceiros** close to **Porto Moniz** (See Walk 33).

.. 25 natural springs cascade into the lake ..

Rounding a bend, we arrive at the amphitheatre where the cliff face towers above us and the 25 natural springs cascade into the small lake at the base of the cliffs (Wp.9 125M) where you can scramble over large boulders in an area of lush green ferns and other indigenous vegetation, so do allow lots of time to soak up the atmosphere and enjoy a rest and refreshments.

Our return route takes us back along the channel for 35 minutes passing the junction (Wp.6 160M) where we joined the *levada*, but instead of climbing back to the forestry post, we continue along **Levada das 25 Fontes** to pick up an alternative path further along. While walking this section, look out for the Madeiran Bilberry (Vaccinium padifolium) which flourishes along here and is a favourite for my family; in late summer we collect the fruit for pies and cakes.

A few minutes later we reach a junction with a path coming up from the right (Wp.10), another route to **Levada da Rocha Vermelha**. We then pass through a rock cutting (Wp.11) before meeting steps ascending on our left where a fingerpost, signed 'Casa do Rabaçal', directs us back to the forestry house (Wp.12 175M).

Signs back to the forest house

But first we can take a short detour by carrying on along the *levada* for another four minutes to reach the **Calheta** tunnel. The area close to the entrance is impressive; to the left water gushes down a channel to feed the *levada*, there's stone seating and lush vegetation around the platform making another ideal picnic spot and also a lovely little shrine set into the rock above the entrance to the tunnel.

Back at the steps, we climb the hillside on our final section of the walk. The pathway is quite rocky in places and we need to duck under horizontal growing tree heaths. It's also quite steep, but there are no dangerous drops and soon we arrive at a junction with more fingerposts.

Straight ahead, but very steep, a path leads up to the forestry house, but going right makes for an easier route on a less steep ascent; I'd suggest the latter though both routes arrive at the picnic area below the house (Wp.13 195M) with tables, chairs and toilets, and more seating in the courtyard at the top of the steps.

.. the lovely well ..

Also worth a mention is the lovely well standing at the top of the yard.

Our trail officially ends at the forestry house; by now you'll probably have had enough climbing, so I suggest the easy option of riding back to the car park on the shuttle bus.

22 RABAÇAL - RIBEIRA GRANDE - LAJEADO - PAÚL DA SERRA

The spectacular gorge of **Ribeira Grande**, across the valley from **Rabaçal**, is a popular destination for walkers with its impressive waterfall and clear blue pool; relax with a picnic, feed the trout or swim during the warmer months.

Pico Rabaçal

This new trail combines the well-trodden route along **Levada do Alecrim** with a much lesser-known trail over **Pico Rabaçal**, making a wonderful circular that takes in forests, mountains and vales. After leaving **Ribeira Grande** we're likely to have the remainder of the route to ourselves to enjoy the peace and tranquility of this beautiful remote area.

The seasons bring striking contrasts; the moorland bracken changes to a copper hue over the winter months. Heaths cover much of the route and in these low forests, giant bilberry trees flourish, their leaves changing to brilliant red during winter.

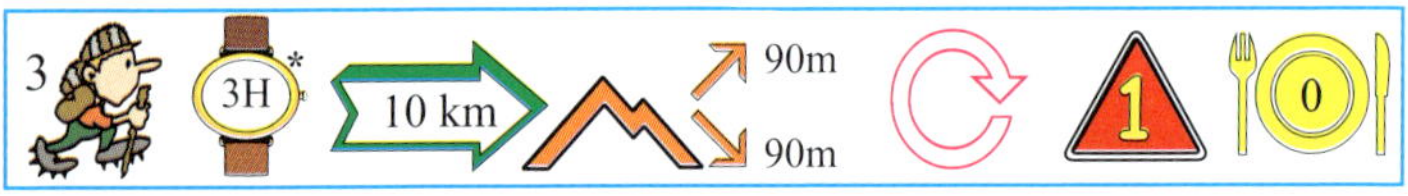

*** + 30 mins detour to Wp.11**

Access by car or taxi:

Follow the ER105 across **Paúl da Serra**; the **Rabaçal** car park is situated approximately 4.5 km west of the **Paúl da Serra** crossroads.

From the road barrier (Wp.1 0M) a path leads off right meeting **Levada do Alecrim** fifty metres ahead; we follow this left (Wp.2 2M). The path is quite stony underfoot and the wide channel shoulder is framed by tree heather which obscures the views for some distance. We arrive at a valley head where **Ribeira do Alecrim** feeds into a water collection pool teeming with trout (Wp.3 13M) and pass over a concrete structure to rejoin the *levada* on the opposite side of the river.

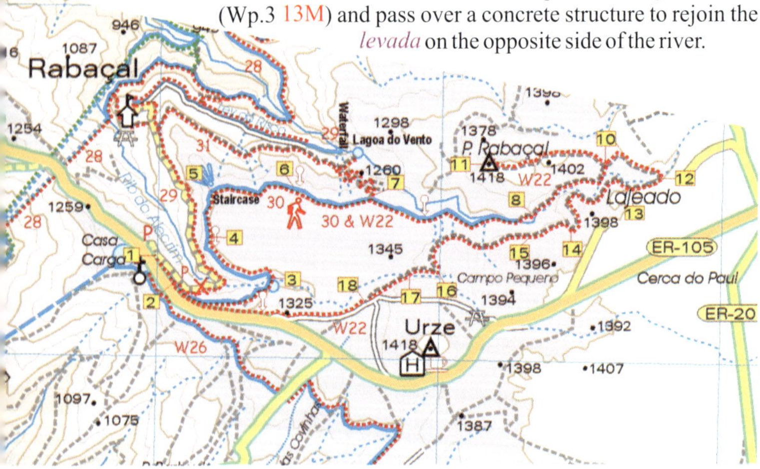

Our route sweeps left, views of the **Janela** valley appearing through breaks in the trees. A little further along, after passing through a couple of rock cuttings (Wp.4 20M) we negotiate one or two precipitous sections, but the path is quite wide and the vegetation gives a sense of security.

Our next milestone is a water stairway (Wp.5 25M) where the *levada* rushes down a steep chute from its higher level. After climbing to the top we're rewarded with more magnificent views down the valley. The channel above the stairway narrows noticeably as it curves towards the **Ribeira Grande** gorge, crossing yet another short unprotected section (Wp.6) before we reach a junction with a path on our left a little further along (Wp.7 40M), the route to **Lagoa do Vento** and the **Rabaçal** forestry post. Ignoring this path, our route continues ahead to arrive at the gorge and waterfall (53M). The pool at the base of the falls is lovely, again teeming with trout and is a wonderful spot worth a break.

Crossing Ribeira Grande

Across the riverbed, our route climbs the banking to reach a rustic stile, first going a few metres to the left before heading off right. The path becomes vague in places but red markers painted on rocks direct us and, as a general rule, we keep to the direction of the river until reaching a path off right leading to the top of the waterfall (Wp.8 61M). Ignoring this path, we veer left and continue to climb dipping under the heaths. Soon the path divides; there are no markers at this point, so when in doubt keep to the lower right hand path. Climbing to the top of a rocky ridge, we can look up the valley; continuing, we follow the line of the river and emerge from the woodland onto a moorland area covered in bracken. The path now becomes much clearer and easier to follow.

Crossing a narrow watercourse (68M) our trail continues close to the river soon reaching more pools and falls (Wp.9 88M). **Pico Rabaçal** is now clearly in view to our left as are the now disused sheep pens ahead in **Lajeado**.

The 30 minute detour to Pico Rabaçal

On Pico Rabaçal

We head directly left to reach the top of the ridge (Wp.10 95M) from where a short detour can be made by following the broad track left to the trig point on **Pico Rabaçal** (1418m). The panoramic views from this vantage point are well worth the effort (Wp.11). Allow an additional 30 minutes return time for this option.

Back on the main trail, we head east along the hillside overlooking the **Lajeado** valley and the car park on the opposite hillside. Around seven minutes ahead, a path descends on our right towards the dry stonewall pens (102M), our next destination. Looking down towards the pens, a grassy track can be seen leading through and along the valley, our onward route to reach a bridge over **Ribeira Lajeado** (Wp.12 109M).

.. like a mountain stream ..

Across the bridge, our route bears right climbing a rough vehicle track. Before reaching the top, another grassy track descends on our right (Wp.13 113M), our route back down to the river and *levada* where we cross a slab over the channel, then follow it left. The channel flows from the riverbed a few metres to our right; we follow it downstream. This lovely *levada*, unlike the traditional irrigation channels on the island, is more like a natural mountain stream with reinforced sections along some of its route. Water-loving plants flourish beside it and trout dash around in its crystal clear waters.

Contouring around the hillside, the *levada* arrives at a waterfall and weir, the river continuing down a stony bed on our right (Wp.14 133M). A new shoulder has been erected around this small valley head, but our route continues over a short section of rough terrain where at times we must scramble over rocks. We reach a rustic stile (Wp.15 139M) and are now in an area of heath forest where Madeira orchids thrive, as do other endemics such as moneywort, Canary buttercups and chrysanthemums.

Fifteen minutes later at the end of the channel (Wp.16 154M), the water is piped, but much falls down into **Ribeira do Alecrim**. Our path heads down to the riverbed before turning right, crossing over the moorland to arrive at a rickety bridge (Wp.17 160M). With not much confidence in this rudimentary structure, it's a good idea to ford the river instead. On the opposite bank a wide track climbs the hillside; at the next junction with a left hand path (Wp.18 169M) the route continues straight ahead, passing a stone marker around 20 metres along from the junction.

After passing a rustic pole signed 'PF' (hunting area) (175M) we again go straight ahead, passing in front of a black stone barn before reaching the ER105 regional road (180M). After following the road right for a short distance, a track on our right (183M) leads us back to our start at the **Rabaçal** car park (Wp.1 185M).

The black stone barn

23 AROUND FANAL

The unique **Fanal** woods and mountains around the forestry post are a magnet for family picnics, barbecues and recreation at weekends and holiday times.. The area surrounding the house could be described as parkland, its pastures populated with groves of centuries-old Madeira laurels; (Fetid Laurel or Til tree *Ocotea foetens*) which have grown to enormous proportions with amazing art forms.

The Fanal mountain area

Fanal woods

This short circular taking in the final section of **PR13 Vereda do Fanal** is an ideal taster for exploring this beautiful area. It also links well with two more of the official walking routes through the **Fanal** forests; **Levada dos Cedros** (**PR14**) and **Vereda da Ribeira da Janela** (**PR15**), make a continuous route from the forestry house to the terraced agricultural parish of **Ribeira da Janela**. (See footnotes for details)

* + extensions

Access by car or taxi:
Follow the ER105 to the **Paúl da Serra** crossroads taking the ER209 signed 'Fanal & Ribeira da Janela'. The Forestry Post is situated on the right hand side of the road, approximately 8.3kms from the junction.

Taking steps on the right of the forestry house (Wp.1 0M) our trail heads up to the flagpoles, going straight ahead before descending to a tarmac road coming up from the forestry driveway. Veering left, the road becomes an earthen track leading us to a wide-open expanse of pastureland criss-crossed with several other tracks. Keeping straight ahead, we follow the central track towards a thicket of trees. As our route ascends, a fingerpost eventually appears indicating 'Fanal 2.2 km', directing us left down a narrow pathway through the vegetation (Wp.2 20M). From this point on the route follows the final section of **Vereda da Fanal**, the **PR13** official walking route - See footnotes for a summary of the full route.

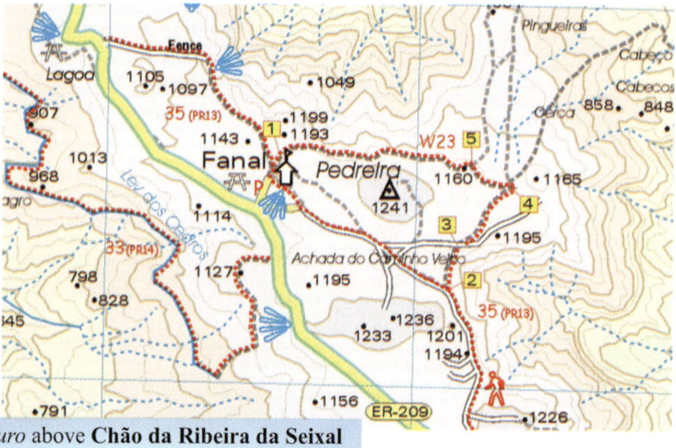

Miradouro above **Chão da Ribeira da Seixal**

There is a short detour from this junction taking us to a lovely *miradouro* overlooking **Chão da Ribeira da Seixal**; continue up the track for a further five minutes taking a left turn onto the viewing platform. Allow around fifteen minutes for this extension.

Back on our route at the 'Fanal 2.2 km' sign, we descend the narrow pathway through the vegetation to reach a junction with another earthen vehicle track (Wp.3 25M) turning right to follow it down to our next fingerpost (Wp.4 40M). At this point our trail is signed left along a narrow path through the undergrowth, soon reaching an old A-framed barn almost hidden in the trees a short distance ahead; another fingerpost (Wp.5 50M) directs us left again to begin a short ascent into the forest. Many more of the ancient Fetid Laurels can be seen along this section - quite spectacular! Endemic species of orchid and Mandon's chrysanthemum can also be seen in summer.

Approaching the knoll

With stunning views down to the northern coastal areas, our path eventually emerges onto a grassy plateau where a splendid high knoll ahead of us dominates the scene, the natural forest sweeping down below us.

Walking through carpets of flowers whilst passing beside two field code markers, our route veers off left along a narrow path before dropping down a logged stairway into the **Fanal** picnic area in the forestry post woodland (Wp.1 75M).

.. amazing Fetid Laurels ..

This is the end of the trail, but allow time here to roam around this charming area before descending the driveway to reach the regional road. Another official information panel close to the gateway gives the telephone number of a local taxi service and for anyone with surplus energy, suggests linking with the following routes:-

PR14 Levada dos Cedros (5.8 kms - Descent 290m - 2¼ hrs one-way)
Built in the 17th century, this is one of the oldest water channels on the island. The route is signed around 300m east of the forestry post on the ER209 from where it descends quite steeply down a logged stairway to reach the source of the *levada*. The trail follows the channel along the right hand slopes of the **Ribeira da Janela** valley passing through a well-conserved section of primitive forest, before ending in **Curral Falso**. **PR15** starts on the opposite side of the regional road.

PR15 Vereda da Ribeira da Janela (2.7kms - Descent 440m - 1¼ hrs one-way)
Following an ancient footpath originally used to connect the northern and southern settlements, this route makes an easy descent into **Ribeira da Janela**, the smallest parish of **Port Moniz**. Predominantly a wine producing area, the village extends from the mouth of the river of the same name to an altitude of 400 metres, its houses scattered among traditional agricultural terraces.

PR13 Vereda do Fanal (10.8 kms - Descent 360m - Ascent 125m - 4hrs one-way)
This magnificent route has excellent pathways and signage throughout. The walk starts on the left of the ER209 regional road 1.2 km from the **Paúl da Serra** crossroads from where the trail undulates over heath moorland frequently dropping into the forested vales and troughs before reaching the forestry post in **Fanal**. The views along the route are spectacular, first looking across to **Rabaçal**, later from the northern escarpment, down to the coastal settlements.

24 TWO WALKS EXPLORING CHÃO DA RIBEIRA PLATEAU - SEIXAL

.. quaint cottages ..

The **Chão da Ribeira** plateau nestles below the **Fanal** mountains high above the north coastal village of **Seixal**. Currently unknown to most tourists and perhaps many residents, it's a wonderful place offering stunning scenery, an educational centre set in the natural forest, quaint cottages, a trout farm and two superb restaurants.

.. weekender accommodation ..

Although predominantly an agricultural area, many of the farm buildings and cottages have been converted into charming weekender accommodation with pretty gardens surrounded by thriving agricultural areas.

The educational centre of **Espaço Natural Floresta Laurissilva** (opened 2007) is situated within the Parque Natural; the tree species are named and there are thatched shelters in the children's themed adventure area. Rustic bridges span babbling streams; there are waterfalls and ponds with water fowl. A signed trail climbs deep into the forest to a magnificent *miradouro* with views over the north coast and up the forested slopes to **Fanal**; maps of the trail can be found in the centre's lovely barbeque restaurant, making this a wonderful day out for all the family.

Mountains surround the plateau

There are two walking routes from **Fanal**, both making steep descents to the plateau, the **Vereda das Voltas** and **Vereda da Cavaca**. But they're difficult trails, so I've chosen two short circulars as tasters. The first starts from the **Laurisilva Restaurant** below the mountain peaks, the second from the **Casa de Pasto Justiniano Restaurant** in the centre of the hamlet.

Access by car or taxi:
Follow the VE2 from **São Vicente** towards **Seixal** and turn left one kilometre before the village onto a narrow road signed 'Chão da Ribeira' which climbs for three kilometres before passing **Bar/Restaurant Casa de Pasto Justiniano** in **Chão da Ribeira**.

800 metres ahead the road turns sharp left at the river; go right here to cross a bridge and continue along a gravel track for 200 metres to reach the car park of **Espaço Natural Floresta Laurissilva** at **Ribeira da Mesa**.

Walk 24A Laurisilva and Riverside

We leave the car park (Wp.1 0M) and head towards the entrance gate of the **Laurisilva Restaurant** where a narrow path leads off to the left, signed 'Vereda das Voltas' (Wp.2). We follow it between agricultural plots and after passing a barn, reach a narrow *levada* channel on our right which soon crosses over to the left (Wp.3 10M). We return to this point to reach the trout farm, but for now continue ahead into the forest.

Many tree species form the forest including Madeira mahogany, Lily of the Valley and Bay Laurels, the latter supporting clumps of Lauribasidium Lauri fungi and only found growing on this species.

Lauribasidium Lauri fungi

It's a green, lush forest; large European ferns sprawl at our feet and endemic flowers scatter the forest floor.

The path ascends, eventually reaching a boulder-strewn river bed (Wp.4 20M). The **Vereda das Voltas** trail continues on the opposite bank, where it begins to climb into the higher forest area; however at this point we turn around and retrace our steps back to the narrow channel (Wp.3) turning right to follow it through the trees to reach a wider fast running channel beside a forest track (Wp.5 35M).

Our route turns right to follow the track, immediately crossing over a cattle grid. With the river to our left, orchards to our right and the mountains closing in around us, we arrive at the driveway of the trout farm, set in lovely gardens (Wp.6 45M). It's possible to buy fresh trout here, but first you need to make arrangements at the **Laurisilva Restaurant**. Stuffed and grilled trout is one of the specialties of the **Casa de Pasto Justiniano Restaurant** and is absolutely delicious.

Our trail continues ahead and at the end of the trout farm boundary, crosses a flat grassy area before the track forks (Wp.7 53M). Going left for a further few minutes leads us to the end of the track beside the wide river bed (Wp.8 60M). The right fork takes us to a large water chute where the channel crosses over a small aqueduct (Wp.9 70M); on the opposite side it's possible to scramble up the banking to reach the *levada*, continuing along it for a short distance.

This is the end of our route, so we return to the trout farm, now following the gravel road back to the car park (Wp.1 90M) for the start of our second circular route from the centre of the hamlet.

Walk 24B Cottages and Flowers

Dropping down the road from the **Espaço Natural Floresta Laurissilva** centre, we reach the **Casa de Pasto Justiniano Restaurant** on our left (Wp.10). This is our starting point where we begin descending the tarred road, passing pretty cottages, gardens, and orchards along the way.

Cottage and crops

Five minutes from the restaurant, as the road starts to descend, we reach and follow the **PR Chão da Ribeira** to **Seixal** on our right (Wp.11 5M) which meanders through a lovely landscape of agricultural plots and cute little cottages.

Two minutes from the road and after crossing a bridge, our route continues towards the forested cliffs now towering on our right as we cross over a rocky stream bed.

Passing a pretty barn

Clusters of barns and cottages occasionally appear and the flora along this trail is superb with Montbretia, Himalayan ginger and the rare endemic Melliferous Spurge in profusion, the latter just coming into flower on our visit here in late May. Soon our first views of the coastline appear and a few minutes later we emerge onto the road beside cottages (Wp.12 17M).

Our trail continues down the tarred road for around 100 metres before it's signed off again to the right where we drop down steps to reach a grassy path (Wp.13 21M). The next sections are a little difficult due to damage from the February 2010 floods, which eroded the pathway which now necessitates a couple of scrambles across the empty water channel.

We ignore a path off to the right, signed 'Sitio do Terra Chá & Paúl da Serra' (another ancient trail over the mountains to **São Vicente** and the south) and continue ahead before emerging again onto the road (Wp.14 32M).

The pathway down to **Seixal** continues across the road (approx. 1km with a 280m descent to the coast) but we leave the trail here and turn left to follow the tarred lane back to our starting point at the **Casa de Pasto Restaurant** (Wp.10 60M). The distance between the two walking routes is just under 1km so allow an additional 15 minutes each way.

25 ESTANQUINHOS to PICO RUIVO DO PAÚL

Paúl da Serra (literally translating to 'swamp of the mountains') is a large plateau on the west of the island covering an area of around 22 km^2. This route, though quite short, is particularly rewarding as it takes in its highest point of **Pico Ruivo do Paúl** (1639 metres above sea level) providing magnificent views in all directions; unsurprisingly, the area is a magnet for walkers and nature lovers, attracting huge numbers of visitors.

Mountain thyme

Our trail crosses a section of **Paúl da Serra** through low shrub land, mainly bracken, broom and gorse, the yellow blossoms magnificent when in bloom. You'll also find carpets of mountain thyme, violets, forget-me-nots and Canary buttercups.

In spring, loud croaking frogs will not fail to attract attention, having colonized the marshy areas close to the path. By taking a little detour they can be spotted as they plop into the water on our approach. Apparently these are Perez's Frog (Rana perezi), similar to Marsh Frogs and the only species found on the island. These were introduced to Madeira in the early 19th century.

Access by car or taxi:
Take the ER105 west from **Encumeada** for approximately 10 kms passing the **Bica da Cana** picnic site on the right.

Around 2 kms ahead, turn right onto the ER208 signed 'Estanquinhos'. Alternatively, approach from the **Paúl da Serra** crossroads (1.6 km) Parking is available close to the junction.

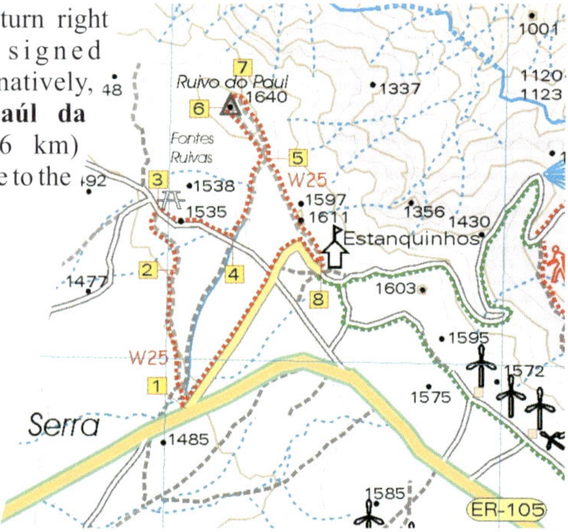

Pico Ruivo do Paúl visible from the start

Starting at the road junction at **Estanquinhos** (Wp.1 0M), we follow a narrow *levada* as it heads northwest over open moorland. **Ruivo do Paúl** can be seen in the distance as it rises up from the bracken, its trig point on the flat summit clearly visible from the start.

Entering the woodland (Wp.2)

The path is quite stony in places, often making progress slow, but after passing beside a number of deciduous trees (Wp.2 10M) our route enters the coniferous woodland, soon arriving at a junction with a broad forest track on the right and the large barbeque area of **Fontes Ruivos** in a clearing straight ahead (Wp.3 20M).

Fingerposts indicate two options; you can either keep following the *levada* to its source close to a water collection pit, then continue on a steep narrow track to the summit of **Ruivo do Paúl** or (our choice), turn right, making a slightly longer but gentler ascent to the summit.

Turning right at this junction, we follow the track through the woodland in the direction of the **Estanquinhos Forestry House**, fifteen minutes along arriving at a junction with another track, this one grassy and leading off left.

The ascent

The fingerpost here indicates the distance to **Pico Ruivo do Paúl** as 0.8km (Wp.4 35M). A short distance along we reach another junction with fingerposts (Wp.5 45M) and going left again, we begin the ascent to the summit.

Around fifty metres from the junction, the track splits, a broad right hand branch heading directly up to a viewing platform on the summit; this will be our return route but for now we continue straight ahead on a narrower path, making a much gentler gradient up the hillside.

Looking back, there are wonderful views of the central mountain range as well as the wind turbines across the plateau, the latter looking quite striking when the light is good.

Keeping the trig point in view our route continues to follow the narrow path towards another fingerpost, soon meeting the alternative steeper path rising up from **Fontes Ruivos**. Joining this track we now turn right to make the final short ascent to the trig point (Wp.6 70M).

On the summit

We are rewarded handsomely for our climb; we are 1639 metres above sea level and enjoy 360° views from this flattish summit. From the viewing platform on the northern escarpment there are magnificent views down the **São Vicente** valley with the full extent of **Paúl da Serra** around us and forested slopes sweeping away in all directions.

.. superb views ..

From here our route crosses to the eastern edge of the summit reaching another fingerpost (Wp.7 90M) which indicates our descent route back to **Estanquinhos** but first, a few metres beyond the sign, we find the second viewing platform, not only with superb views of the north coast but also views of the central massif.

Making a steep descent back to the junction at (Wp.5) and ignoring our inward route to this point, we now continue straight ahead on a narrow grassy path towards **Estanquinhos** and the ER208. Along this final section, the trail passes through another area of coniferous woodland before eventually reaching the forestry house (Wp.8 105M).

Turning right and descending the drive for 25 metres takes us to the ER208, the tarred access road leading up from the ER105. It's then around 1km along this road back to our starting point (Wp.1 120M).

26 LEVADA DO PAÚL - CRISTO REI TO FATIMA CHAPEL, RABAÇAL

Southern views

The narrow channel of **Levada do Paúl** flows along open moorland where pale green hills sweep away below us giving way to darker forested areas. On clear days there are wonderful views of the southern coastline with **Achada de Santo Antão** at

.. cattle roam freely ..

Arco da Calheta first in view. Undoubtedly we'll meet other walkers as we progress along this well-trodden route; it's also a grazing area for the cattle that roam freely around these hillsides so don't be surprised to find them on the pathway; fortunately they're not obstructive so it's simply a matter of being patient and allowing them to pass.

Access by car or taxi:
Follow the ER105 from the **Encumeada** pass to the **Paúl da Serra** crossroads, turning left onto the ER209. After a further 3 kms, turn right into the car park beside the **Cristo Rei** statue.

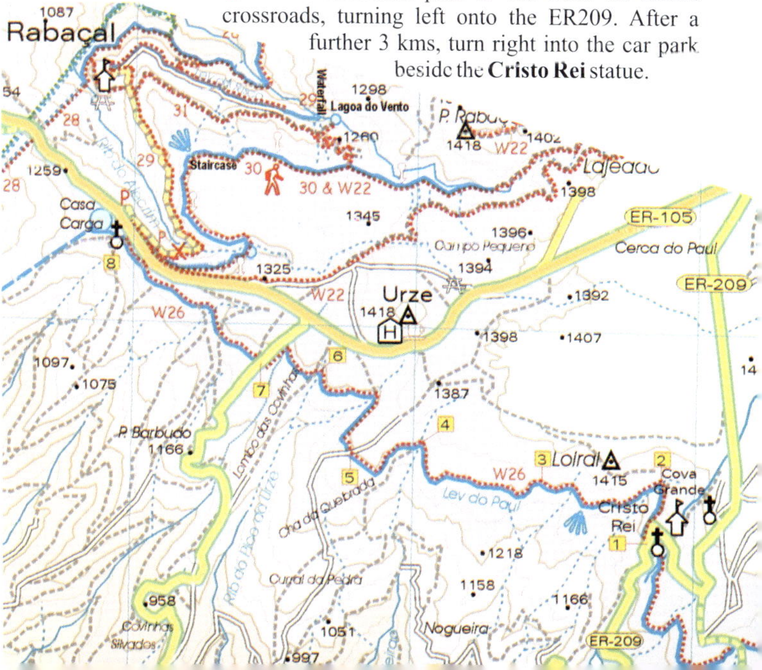

Leaving the car park, we follow the ER209 downhill for a short distance to where the channel crosses under the road just after a right hand bend. Here we turn right, following the *levada* downstream (Wp.1 0M). Our route immediately heads into the first valley and with wind turbines above us, we round its head to ford a pretty stream on stepping-stones (Wp.2 10M). The river tumbles down its rocky bed before dropping into a small gorge to our left. A few minutes along we arrive at the second waterfall (Wp.3 30M), after which the terrain becomes much rockier, the contrasts of this pleasant moorland changing with the seasons, the bright green bracken and yellow broom and gorse of spring and summer, autumn colours prevailing in winter.

.. an ideal place for lunch ..

The third waterfall (Wp.4 40M) with its little weir and clear pool provides a lovely setting for a rest or lunch. After leaving this pretty spot and crossing over a moorland track (Wp.5 50M), we reach intriguing caves dug into the rocky hillside (Wp.6 70M), beyond which the *levada* becomes a corridor between tall broom before snaking once again round open hillside, arriving at the new regional road leading down to **Arco da Calheta** (Wp.7 80M).

The reservoir

Another twenty minutes brings us alongside the pretty chapel of **Nossa Senhora de Fátima** and, just to the left, a reservoir that feeds the hydropower station in **Calheta**; we climb a path beside this to cross over to the **Rabaçal** *miradouro* and car park (Wp.8 105M). A short distance east from the **Rabaçal** carpark you'll find the Jungle Rain bar, restaurant and tourist shop, a good place to visit and watch the world go by.

If you wish to return to the starting point from here, you can rejoin the channel a short distance down the new **Arco** road.

Cristo Rei

Cristo Rei Statue

The white marble statue of **Cristo Rei** was erected in 1962. Also known as **Nosso Senhor da Montanha** (Our Lord of the Mountain) the area is surrounded by trees and terracing, creating a little oasis in this moorland area. Below the statue stands a large arch, other sculptures and a spring, plus a number of stone plinths inscribed with religious proverbs.

27 CRISTO REI - LEVADA DA BICA DA CANA

Levada da Bica da Cana

Another route from **Cristo Rei**, this time taking us in an easterly direction following **Levada da Bica da Cana**. It's an exhilarating walk along this narrow channel which eventually leads us into the mountains, yet the terrain is comfortable and the views just get better and better as you progress along.

There's also the option of combining this trail with Walk 6 to make a continuous route via **Cascalho** to **Boca da Encumeada**. (See footnote for details).Note: this route was closed at the time of publication for repair work.

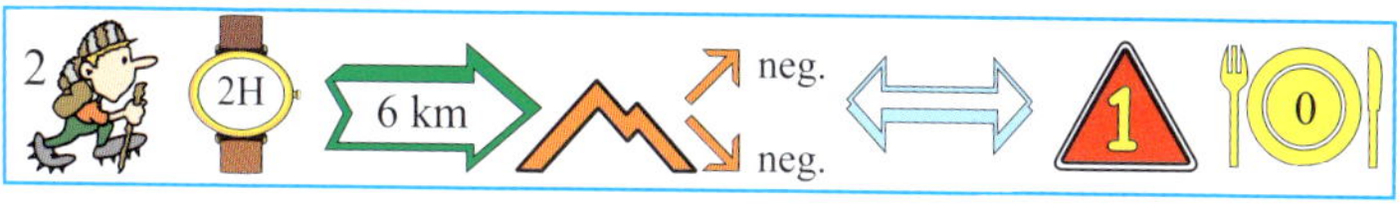

Access by car or taxi:
Follow the ER105 from the **Encumeada** pass to the **Paúl da Serra** crossroads turning left onto the ER209. After a further 3 kms, turn right into the car park beside the **Cristo Rei** statue or park on the roadside a little further down.

Dropping down the road from the statue, **Levada do Paúl** crosses in front of an old water house standing on our left, before disappearing under the road on its route to **Rabaçal**. We follow the channel east passing in front of the house and through a rock cutting to arrive at a stream bed. Here the two channels separate and we now follow **Levada da Bica da Cana** upstream. (Wp.1 0M).

Moving along the clay and grass path where gorse and broom abound, another channel soon appears crossing diagonally before continuing down the

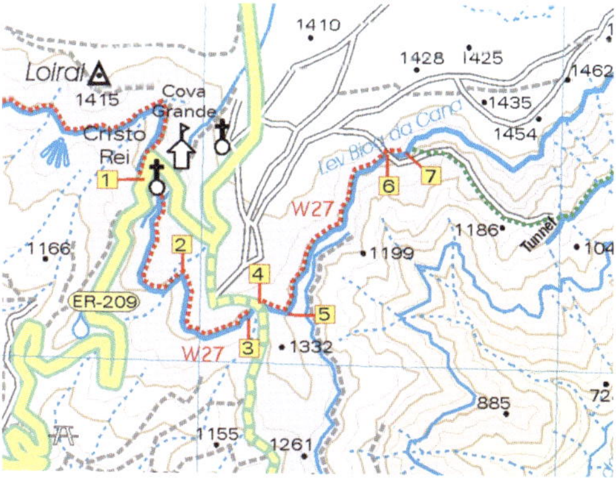

hillside; just beyond, we reach a valley head crossing over a water run-off (Wp.2 10M). Our path snakes along the moorland, occasionally crossing small becks and springs and as we stroll along we take in the superb views down to the southern villages and coastline.

.. a huge pine stands in isolation ..

Rounding the next hillside, deep slopes appear on our right with coniferous forest lying in the valley bottom and, along this barren ridge, we arrive at a spot ideal for a picnic, where a huge pine stands in isolation, quite striking (Wp.3 22M).

Three minutes ahead we reach a T-junction with a cobbled lane coming down from the left and descending into the valley on our right (Wp.4 25M). On the opposite side of the track the *levada* can be seen coursing down a slope; we cross the track and ascend to a cairn and a magnificent viewpoint at the top of the slope (Wp.5 29M).

.. endemic giant sow thistles ..

We are now standing on a mountain pass high above the **Ponta da Sol** valley and are looking across to the **Encumeada** pass; it's spectacular!

Our route turns left and passes over a stile before continuing along the hillside. The path becomes quite wet and muddy in places and the shoulder narrows, though there's lots of vegetation for protection. Endemic giant sow thistles grow along this section flowering during the summer months.

High above the valley

The route becomes more beautiful and remote as we continue deeper into the valley.

Towards the end we must negotiate a couple of narrow and exposed sections of shoulder, also hampered by overhanging rock; nevertheless these short sections are passable with care and we soon continue again along the grassy pathway (see photo over page).

The rocky section

As we approach the valley head, an earthen track can be seen descending the valley with the narrow channel climbing up the hillside ahead. The track is the route down to **Cascalho**; the channel comes down the hillside bringing the waters of *levada* **Bica da Cana** from their source.

We arrive at the T-junction with the track (Wp.6 52M), so those planning to walk through to **Cascalho** and on to **Boca da Encumeada** should leave the trail here; our route continues for a few minutes along the channel on the opposite side of the track.

The next section is narrow and we have to negotiate a waterfall bursting over the *levada*, but the shoulder is well constructed and the surface even, so we can easily pass along for another few minutes until the channel veers left (Wp.7 57M). At this point we turn around and retrace out steps back to **Cristo Rei** (Wp.1 120M).

Extension to Cascalho and Boca da Encumeada (Total route 12km - 4 hrs one-way)

There are two choices here; firstly, to follow the track to **Cascalho** and then return by the same route back to **Cristo Rei**, or to continue on to **Encumeada**. The track drops down the valley on a 350m descent taking you to the source of the **Ponta do Sol** river; here waterfalls cascade down over a rock-walled amphitheatre. It's quite an exposed area but it is fenced and passable with care. En-route this trail passes through three tunnels, the longest of which is around 3 km and takes 1 hour to negotiate.

Important Note: This continuous route was closed at the time of publication due to landslides, so anyone wishing to walk to **Encumeada** should first contact the tourist offices to ascertain the status of the trail before setting out.

28 BICA DA CANA - PINÁCULO - CIRCULAR

Bica da Cana is a popular weekend picnic site for local people, when entire families spend the day barbecuing and relaxing in the woodland beside the forestry house. Our circular route heads firstly to the *miradouro* and trig point (1620m) with breathtaking views of the central massif, then drops into an area of natural forest along **Levada da Serra** lying on the north-eastern edge of the **Paúl da Serra** plateau. We take in a tranquil lunch spot at the foot of **Pináculo**, often referred to as Madeira's '**Sugar Loaf Mountain**' due to its elliptical shape, then return to the starting point along a section of the official **PR17 Caminho do Pináculo e Folhadal** trail high above the **São Vicente** valley. (See footnote for details of this additional walking route).

There's plenty of botanical interest as the trail passes through areas of *laurisilva* and heath forest where endemic species thrive.

Sow thistles, Canary buttercups and Bilberry grow to huge proportions whilst Madeira orchids, wild geraniums, Mandon's chrysanthemum, mountain stock and stonecrops provide rich colour from spring through to autumn. Along the damper habitats of the *levada*, water dropwort, navelwort, liverworts and ferns flourish.

Madeira orchids

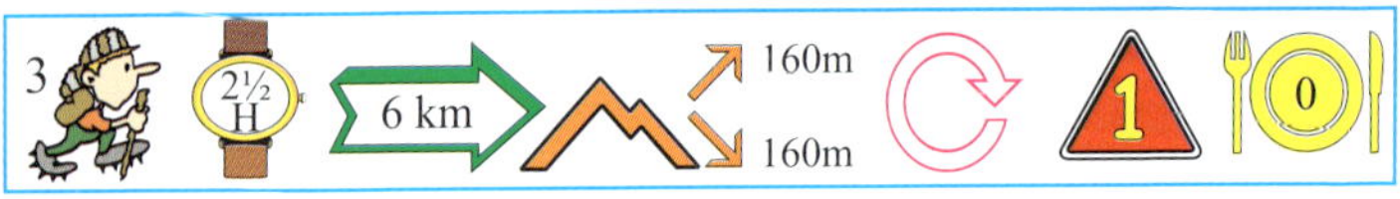

Access by car or taxi:
Take the VE4 north from **Ribeira Brava**, turning left on the ER105 for **Serra da Agua** and **Encumeada**. On reaching the summit, the road forks sharp left, continuing for around 8 km through the mountain pass; the forestry house and car park of **Bica da Cana** are located on the right of the road.

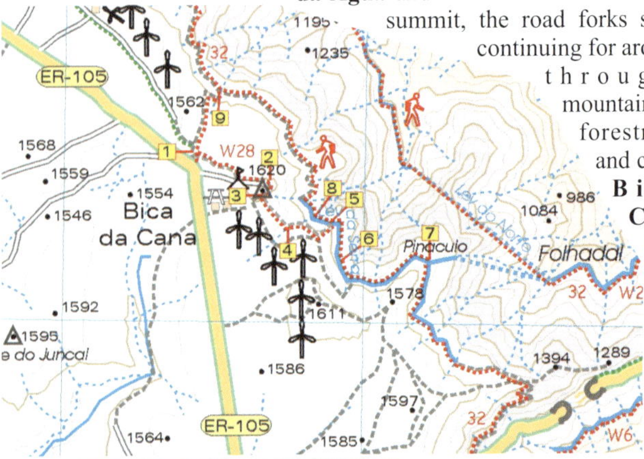

From the north and west, approach from the **Paúl da Serra** crossroads taking the ER105 east for 4.5 km.

From the main gateway (Wp.1 0M) we follow a cobbled path veering left off the vehicle track to climb to the *miradouro* (Wp.2 12M) to take in spectacular views of Madeira's highest peaks; **Pico Ruivo** and **Pico do Areeiro** are in front of us, whilst the basalt outcrop of **Pináculo** is in sight lower down the valley.

The descent to Pináculo (after Wp.3)

Passing beside picnic tables, we head up to the trig point (Wp.3 16M) before taking a clearly defined path on the far left to descend in the direction of the wind turbines. We walk alongside a fence then reach a broken stile on our right (Wp.4 26M), immediately turning left and following a water channel for a few metres before crossing over it to continue our descent through the heather.

We pass a cairn before eventually emerging onto the shoulder of **Levada da Serra**, our route for the moment going right to follow the channel downstream (Wp.5 41M), although we return to this spot after visiting **Sugar Loaf**.

.. a waterfall crashes down ..

Heading towards **Pináculo** the aqueduct has been carved between the rock face and the mountain slopes of the **São Vicente** valley. Now on a section of the official **PR17** route, we pass a number of semi circular rock walls where water sprays into the channel, stunning when caught in the sunlight. The largest of these resembles a small amphitheatre; here a waterfall crashes down over the *levada* (Wp.6 50M) so a raincoat might be a bonus at this point.

.. more views of Sugar Loaf ..

We push through lush yellow masses of flowering broom that often dominate the path. With more views of **Sugar Loaf** and the high peaks appearing through the vegetation, we eventually arrive at the base of **Pináculo**

(Wp.7 62M), a lovely quiet place with stone seating, ideal for a stop or refreshments.

The **PR17** route arrives at **Sugar Loaf** on a paved pathway coming up from the right of our path just beyond the seating area (see footnote for summary of this official walking trail).

Our signed ascent to Bica da Cana

Back on our main route, we retrace our steps, passing the junction where we joined the *levada* and continuing along the channel shoulder in a westerly direction. We eventually reach a short flight of steps on our left leading up to a waterfall (Wp.8 102M).

Ignoring these, our route begins to undulate as we continue along the *levada* and pathway for a further twenty minutes to reach a fingerpost directing us left back to **Bica da Cana** (Wp.9 127M). The **PR17** continues on to **Encumeada** from this point.

Leaving the *levada* at the fingerpost, we ascend a rocky stairway twisting up the hillside. Eventually the vegetation thins out as we continue to ascend, following the fence and tree line until arriving back on the ER105 at our starting point (Wp.1 150M).

PR17 Caminho do Pináculo e Folhadal

This beautiful trail, beginning on the ER105 at **Lombo do Mouro**, climbs 170m up the escarpment before following **Levada da Serra** below **Bica da Cana**. Descending first along an ancient footpath, later on a broad vehicle track at **Caramujo**, the trail arrives in **Folhadal** where it picks up **Levada do Norte**, the final section passing through six tunnels on its route back to **Encumeada**.

29 ENCUMEADA - FOLHADAL - GINHAS, SÃO VICENTE

Leaving Encumeada

From a magnificent start at **Encumeada** we follow **Levada do Norte** to **Folhadal** before dropping down a forest track to reach another fantastic water channel above **São Vicente**. Although this trail takes in only a very short section of **Levada da Fajã do Rodrigues**, there is an option to add these two stunning walks together.

Our trail to **Ginhas** passes through exotic primeval forest in the area of **Folhadal**, named after the endemic Folhados - lily of the valley trees (Clethra arborea), one of the most common trees in this area. Growing to a maximum of seven metres, it displays masses of upright clusters of fragrant white flowers between August and October.

Lily of the Valley tree

However, you need to have your torches ready as the trail negotiates six en-route tunnels carved through the mountains. Whilst these make for uncomfortable walking as there is no wall between the path and channel, they are reasonably dry and level underfoot and any discomfort is well worth the effort. But do take them slowly; the water is quite deep, cold and fast flowing. Closed for quite a long period following damage from the 2010 floods, the channel has now been repaired and reinstated to a high standard to prevent similar problems in the future; sturdy posts and wire have also been erected on all difficult sections.

Access by car or taxi:
Follow the directions given for Walk 6 to the starting point at **Boca da Encumeada**. Parking is available around the gift shop on the ER105.

Access by bus:
Rodoeste buses N°6 and N°139 from **Funchal** and **Ribeira Brava** serve **Boca da Encumeada**. There's also a limited bus service from **Ginhas** to **São Vicente** picking up the Rodoeste routes for your return journey.

Dropping down the road from the gift shop (Wp.1 0M) and turning right towards the **Encumeada Snack Bar**, we find the channel on the opposite side of the road at the top of a short flight of steps (Wp.2 3M).

This is the beginning of the **PR17** trail via **Folhadal**, **Caramujo** and **Bica da Cana**; there's an information panel at the top of the steps (see footnote for details). It's also the starting point for our Walk 6 route and so we follow the *levada* to Wp.3 of that route where we then turn right, following **Levada do Norte** into the first tunnel (Wp.3 23M).

The shortest tunnel at Wp.5

The tunnel entrance and first section are quite narrow but it gets easier further along and takes just over fifteen minutes to walk through. On emerging (Wp.4 40M), both vegetation and climate are noticeably different now, it's usually much cooler on this northern side as well as wild and green.

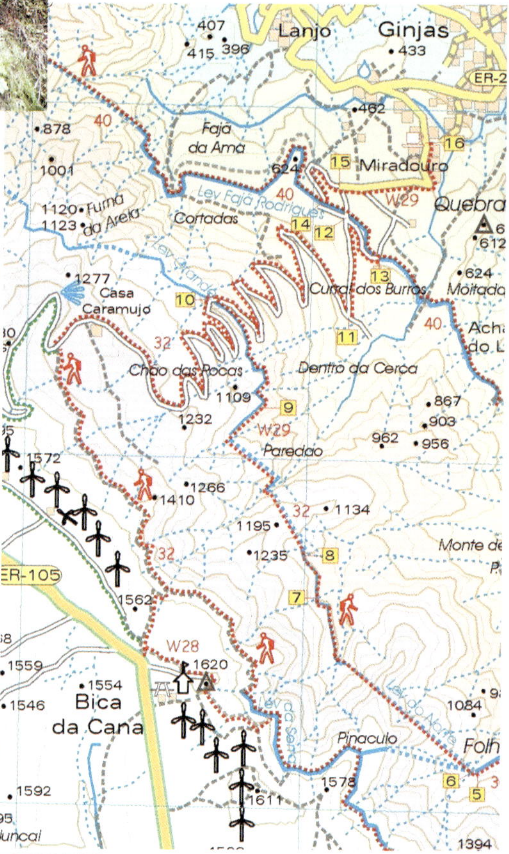

The next tunnel (Wp.5 55M) is really more of an arch and requires no torch though it is soon followed by the longest tunnel at 1 kilometre (Wp.6 60M); there's quite a spectacular waterfall to the left dropping down around 100 metres.

This tunnel has reasonable headroom, but is narrow in places and there are a few short areas where the shoulder has been eroded, so the motto again is to take it slowly. Around the half way mark you also become aware of an eerie noise but don't be alarmed, it's only the echo of a water chute feeding into the *levada* at the exit. This third tunnel takes just over twenty minutes to pass through.

Sweet violets

Now becoming accustomed to this environment, we can take time to look for the wonderful flora around us. Orchids, sweet violets, geraniums, mountain stock, giant buttercups, chrysanthemum and pride of Madeira all grow along this section as does the rare endemic Melliferous spurge (Euphorbia mellifera); the latter flowering between February and August.

Ten minutes along we pass steps dropping sharp right (Wp.7 94M), we ignore these and continue to follow the channel. A few metres ahead the shoulder is narrow and unprotected for a short distance.

The fourth tunnel (300 metres taking around 14minutes) (Wp.8 104M) and the fifth (200 metres taking around 10 minutes) are only a few metres apart, but once at the end, breathe a sigh of relief, the final tunnel (Wp.9 134M) is only around 10 metres in length and requires no torch.

Casa dos Lavaceiros and Levada do Norte

Another 18 minutes along we arrive at the lovely water house (**Casa dos Lavaceiros**) sitting beside the channel (Wp.10 152M), a good place to take a rest or a lunch break.

We leave the *levada* at this point where it crosses under a wide forest track. Going right, we begin a long descent towards **Ginhas**.

This forest track leads down from **Estanquinhos Forestry Post** on **Paúl da Serra** to **Ginhas** above **São Vicente**; the construction of the road destroyed the original path and the surrounding forest. So it's a bit of slog from here for a while but is compensated by some lovely views along the way.

Reaching a T-junction (Wp.11 203M), our route swings left. Continuing down the track for another twenty minutes brings us to a crossroads of tracks (Wp.12 226M) where we turn right, passing between two houses. Just ahead at another junction, our track bends left taking us down to **Levada da Fajã do Rodrigues** (Wp.13 234M).

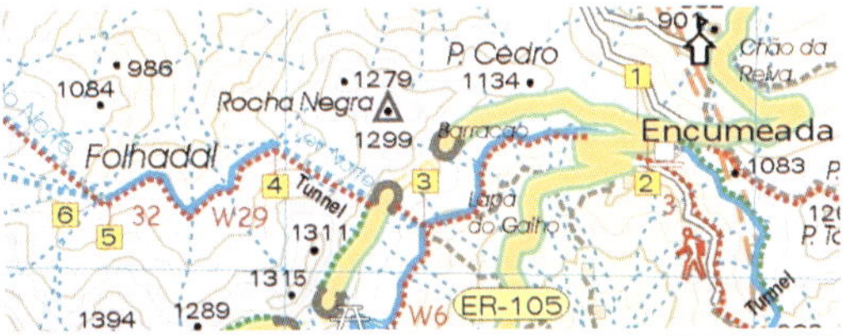

Turning left and following the channel upstream, we pass through a very pretty agricultural area, the channel shoulder planted with exotic flowers.

Just less than ten minutes along we arrive at the **PR16** information panel (Wp.14 244M). Anyone wishing to join up these two walks, or to do a short section of this *levada* (the views along the first fifteen to twenty minutes stretch are spectacular) should cross over the track to pick up the channel on the opposite side. (See footnote for details of this extension).

Now dropping down the wide track which soon swings sharp right, we arrive at a tarred road and junction with the Industrial Park road (Wp.15 250M). Going straight ahead along the tarred road will lead us to **Bar Miradouro** in **Ginhas** for a well-earned drink (Wp.16 270M); the views of the eastern mountain range from **Ginhas** are spectacular.

The eastern slopes, from Ginhas

The proprietors will gladly call a taxi from this point, alternatively call the local driver on 291 842 238. Bus stops can be found around one kilometre ahead in the village centre or on the old **São Vicente** road.

Extension along PR16 Levada da Fajã do Rodrigues to Ribeira do Inferno (3 hours return - 7.8 kilometres)
This *levada* leads into one of the rarest areas of the *laurisilva*, enabling us to penetrate an area of the interior otherwise inaccessible. The route makes an exhilarating trail along a mountainous ledge with magnificent views most of the way. But the downside is that there are four more difficult tunnels along this *levada* before arriving in one of the most amazing areas on the island. So, it may be best to leave this for another day, but whenever you walk this route I guarantee you won't be disappointed. (See Walk 40 in Walk! Madeira published by Discovery Walking Guides for full walking notes of this route).

PR17 - Encumeada - Pináculo - Folhadal (14 kms - 5½ hours)
Beginning at **Lombo do Mouro**, approximately three kilometres from the **Encumeada** gift shop on the ER105, this trail takes us up a rugged stairway to join **Levada da Serra** leading us through beautiful forest to **Pináculo** below **Bica da Cana**. Later passing through **Caramujo**, the **PR17** continues on to **Encumeada** following **Levada do Norte** in reverse of our trail above. (See Walk 32 - Walk! Madeira for the full walking notes on this route).

Note: After the Feb 2010 flood, a section of this route between **Lombo do Mouro** and **Pináculo** was closed and remained so at the time of publication (Sept 2011). Anyone wishing to walk this entire trail should therefore check the status with one of the Tourist Offices before setting out.

30 SANTA - PORTO MONIZ

This short yet stunning walk takes in spectacular views of the north coast to be enjoyed by everyone who can manage the descent. Beginning close to the paroquial church of **Santa**, our route follows **Caminho do Pico**, an ancient cobbled trail zigzagging down the cliffs into the pretty town of **Porto Moniz**.

One of the most popular north coast tourist locations, **Porto Moniz** is probably best known for its outstanding natural seawater swimming pool, now expanded along the whole of the sea front.

São João Fort

In addition, the town has undergone substantial development over the last few years, accommodating many new hotels, restaurants and shops; it's also home to a new *aquário* housed in the lovely old **São João Fort**, as well as a new living science museum, the **Ciéncia Viva Centre**. Add to this the pretty harbour with its colourful fishing boats and the stunning coastal views; it's not surprising that visitors flock here throughout the year.

Porto Moniz harbour

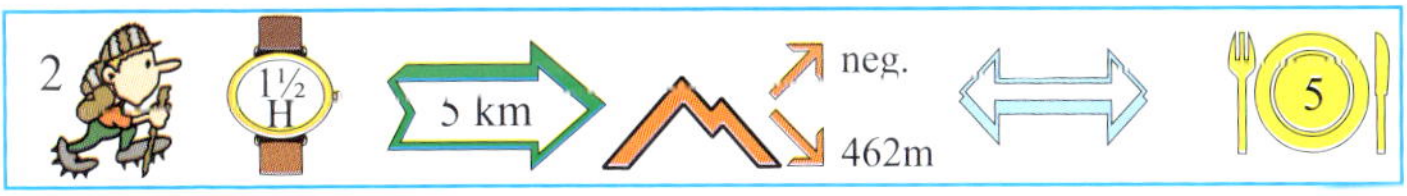

Access by hire car or taxi:
Take the regional ER105 across **Paúl da Serra** to the junction with the ER 101 at **Portas da Vila**. Turning right, follow the signs for 'Porto Moniz' and continue for 1.8 kms to the village of **Santa**, parking close by the church.

Access by bus:
Bus routes 80, 139, & 150 from **Funchal** service the **Porto Moniz** and **Santa** areas but are irregular and slow, therefore are not recommended.

Leaving the church in **Santa** (Wp.1 0M) we descend the regional road for a few metres before taking a tarred lane leading off to the left (Wp.2 3M), a few minutes later arriving at a crossroads (Wp.3 10M). Going straight ahead to follow **Caminho do Pico**, we stroll through a gentle agricultural area before the road surface changes to a concrete lane and starts a very steep descent.

Whilst it's quite tough on the knees along this stretch, we're rewarded with

superb views of **Ilhéu Mole** islet with its pretty lighthouse as well as the harbour and the seawater pools of **Porto Moniz**. Eventually we arrive at a *miradouro* where the lane finally ends at a turning circle (Wp.4 33M).

To our right, steps lead us onto the ancient cobbled trail. After passing beside a house on the cliff top we begin snaking down the hillside, taking in dramatic views of the ER101 with its hairpin bends and patchwork of tiny fields while to the south, *laurisilva* forested slopes complete this picturesque scene.

Rock Navelwort

The vegetation along the descent is typical of the rugged north-western cliffs, supporting Giant Reeds, Houseleeks and Globe Flowers with Corn Poppies, Sea-Stocks and Sow Thistles providing stunning contrast. Rock Navelwort (Umbilicus rupestris), a species mostly confined to the *laurisilva*, can also be spotted growing in the clefts of rocks and walls along this route, its tall dense flowers appearing in early summer.

Soon the path drops into denser vegetation in the valley bottom before crossing a small stream and heading towards the outskirts of the old town.

Remnants of past cultivation remain, with Mango, Fig and Loquat trees flanking the route and a narrow *levada* flowing on our right. Eventually the cobbled track comes to an end at a junction with a newly tarred road leading from the ER101.

Porto Moniz as seen from the old town

Our route goes left, though a short detour to the right will bring us to **Snack Bar A Latada** (Wp.5 63M), across from which is a wonderful *miradouro* providing fantastic view of the whole of the town and coastline.

Back on our route, we descend the tarred road lined with new and older properties and small vineyards and soon, after a sharp right hand bend, we leave the tarred road on a steep concrete lane which takes us into a small square.

Approaching Nossa Sra. da Cóncéicão church

Following the sign for 'Caminho Pedro Mole' (Wp.6 68M), we pass along a quaint cobbled alleyway running between charming cottages with lovely gardens, where Wisteria hangs over the garden walls, the spire of **Porto Moniz** church dominating the vista ahead. This attractive 17th century church built by Francisco Moniz is dedicated to Nossa Sra. da Concéicão. As we approach the building, a newly-paved pathway leads us between the church and a charming well and into the town's municipal square (Wp.7 71M).

Taking the ER101 regional road on our final section, we descend into the town, soon turning left following a sign for 'Piscinas' (swimming pools) (Wp.8 80M) and as we arrive at a junction in front of the post office (Wp.9 87M) our route turns right leading us to the sea front with it vast selection of bars, restaurants and gift shops (Wp.10 90M).

Buses and taxis are available from the centre as well as from the municipal square to take us back to our starting point; a taxi will cost around €10. An alternative for the more energetic of course, is to retrace your steps back along **Caminho do Pico** to the starting point at **Santa** church.

31 PONTA DO PARGO to CABO

This walk along country lanes makes a lovely alternative to *levada* and mountain trails and here one can stride out, take in the views and soak up the atmosphere of this tranquil area in the west of the island. Please refer to Walk 34 for further information on **Ponta do Pargo**.

Capela Nossa Senhora do Boa Morte

The route passes through a number of hamlets before arriving at **Cabo**, perhaps the prettiest headland on the island with its striking white chapel and grassy promontory to the cliff edge. There are also two detours along the route, one to a trig point on the cliffs with more splendid views along the coastline, another to an old school house in **Lombo Quinedo** where a tiny shrine sits snugly in an enormous eucalyptus tree.

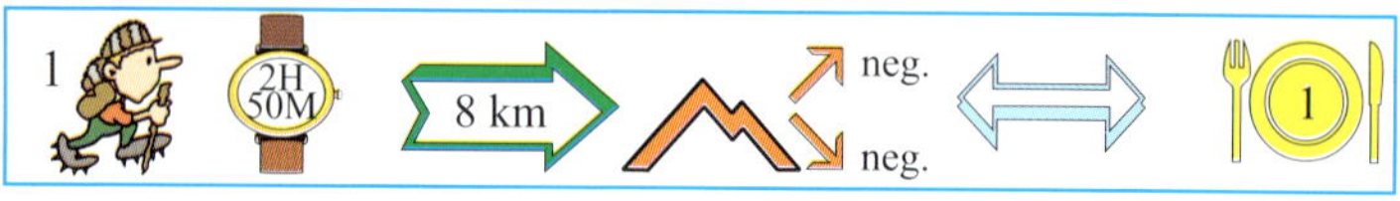

Access by hire car or taxi:
Follow the VE3 and ER101 to **Ponta do Pargo** taking the second left signed 'Pico das Favas'. A few metres ahead you reach a junction with the village road and a sign post on the right for **Caminho Velha**. This is our route to **Cabo**. Park around this junction

Access by bus:
N°142 departs from **Funchal**, though return times are not convenient.

From our start at the village junction (Wp.1 0M) we follow **Caminho do Velha**, a concrete lane descending off to the right running almost parallel to the ER101. The road dips into the valley, climbing on its opposite side to reach **Pedregal**, a pretty hamlet of traditional buildings with well tended gardens offering magnificent displays of Wisteria and Jasmine in spring.

We pass a drinking well on our right (Wp.2 20M) - the first of many along this route - then a junction with a road off right which we ignore, continuing along the country lane to reach a cross roads in the hamlet of **Serrado** where we go straight ahead, passing another well on our right (Wp.3 30M). The traditional Portuguese houses here are noteworthy; many are derelict and abandoned, but displaying elegant and ornate carvings around the doors and windows.

.. displaying elegant and ornate carvings ..

Leaving this hamlet and following **Caminho do Velha**, the road now bends

A cow tethered alongside the route

right and descends, passing yet another drinking fountain on the right (Wp.4 36M). A few minutes ahead we cross a bridge over **Ribeira da Vaca** (river of the cows), aptly

The old schoolhouse

named in this farming area (Wp.5 41M). From the river, our route then ascends into **Lombo Quinedo**. A large palm tree announces the start of the hamlet; to the left is the old derelict schoolhouse building and a copse of large date palms.

Turning first left beside an impressive new house (Wp.6 46M) takes us to a pretty little shrine set into the trunk of an enormous eucalyptus tree in front of the old building. Turning back onto **Caminho do Velha**, our route leaves **Lombo Quinedo**, making another short ascent to the next hamlet of **Lombada Velha**, another drinking well appearing on our right (Wp.7 52M). As the lane ascends through the village, look out for a left turn beside a house, signed 'Capela' (Wp.8 56M), a short tarred road which becomes a wide earthen track after the second house. The track leaves the village behind and contours around a small valley of low shrub land.

We reach a cross road of earthen tracks (Wp.9 65M); left will be our exit route from the trig point at **Vermelho**, which we'll take on our return journey, but for now we continue in the direction of **Cabo**. Passing a second track off to the left (Wp.10 68M), our detour route to the trig point, we continue ahead for a few metres and on approaching a sparse woodland of eucalyptus and pine, we take in our first view of **Capela Nossa Senhora do Boa Morte**,

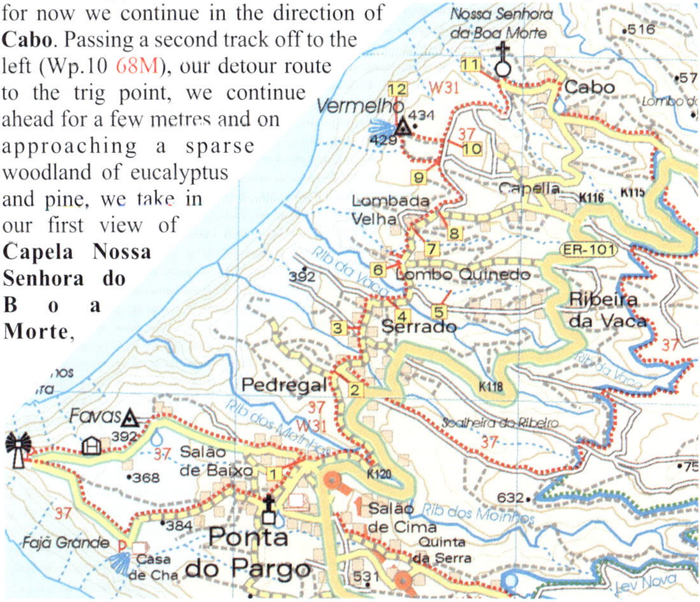

The headland at Cabo

the solitary white chapel at **Cabo**. There are two routes to it; one dropping into the valley just before the track bends right and our route, which maintains height and continues around the valley head before arriving at the car park beside the chapel (Wp.11 80M), a beautiful spot above the headland. The original early 17th century chapel, now rebuilt, retains many original features, the architectural style typical Portuguese.

It's well worth a visit to see the Baroque altar and lovely furninshings (check at the church in **Ponta do Pargo** for opening times). From the chapel, a narrow concrete path can be seen heading across the low grassy promontory leading to a *miradouro* on the cliff edge allowing fine views along the coastline and an ideal place for a picnic.

.. wonderful views ..

Our return from **Cabo** back to the starting point is by the same route, but around twelve minutes from the chapel, back at (Wp.10), we turn right to make a short detour to the trig point of **Vermelho**. The path drops down for a short distance, reaching a T-junction with a track coming down from the left. Here we turn right and follow a short incline to the cliff edge (Wp.12 97M) - the views are stunning.

A few metres to the left we can look east, back to the **Ponta do Pargo** lighthouse, but care is needed here as there is no protective fencing along these cliffs. From the cliff edge a number of paths rejoin the track at the T-Junction, our route now continuing straight ahead to return to our main track (Wp.9 103M). Going right, we return to the hamlet of **Lombada Velha** before continuing the final stretch of our journey via **Serrado** and **Pedregal** back to the start (Wp.1 170M).

Extension: (Allow 1 hour return)
Once back in **Ponta do Pargo** we can extend this route by visiting the lighthouse and *miradouro* at **Casa de Chá**. The original road descending around **Pico das Favas** has been closed due to the construction of the road network for the new golf course. As a result, take the village road across to the church and from there follow the signs for 'O Farol' and 'Miradouro'. Open to the public daily, the lighthouse provides information on this location and gives presentations on other lighthouses around the archipelago. The tea shop of **Casa de Chá** is open daily throughout the year (not Mondays and throughout February).

32 LEVADA DO MOINHO - PORTAS DA VILA - ACHADAS DA CRUZ

This trail, part of the official **PR7** route, follows a section of **Levada do Moinho** (The Mill Route) which opened to the public in 2008 and is as yet unknown to most visitors, so we may well have it all to ourselves. The full route of 10.3 kilometres runs from **Ribeira da Cruz**, close to the boundary of **Calheta** and **Porto Moniz**, to **Junqueira**, **Lamaceiros** where the well-known route of **Levada da Ribeira da Janela** begins (See Walk 33).

Our trail passes through one of the best preserved sections of the *laurisilva* on the north-west of the island, taking us along a spectacular walk with waterfalls, ravines, pools and sub-tropical vegetation, finally leading us to an ancient water mill at **Achadas da Cruz**.

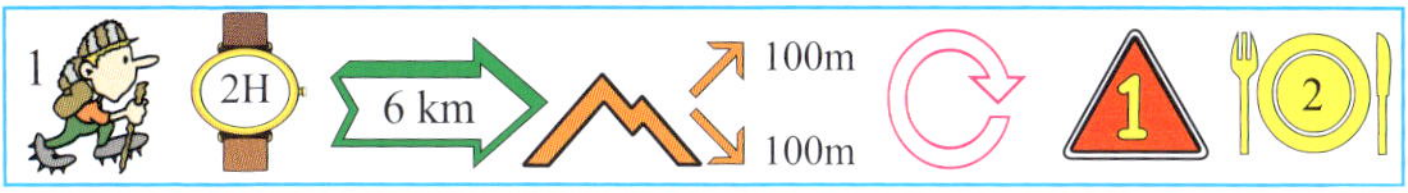

Access by car or taxi:
Take the ER105 over **Paúl da Serra** to reach the T-junction with the ER101 at **Portas da Vila**, **Santa** (a few kilometers above **Porto Moniz**). Parking is available along the roadside next to the **Posto Florestal da Santa** forestry house.

Access by bus:
Bus routes 80, 139 & 150 from **Funchal** service the **Porto Moniz** / **Santa** areas though are irregular and slow so are therefore not recommended.

The fingerpost at Wp.1

On the opposite side of the road from the forestry house a finger post, signed 'Ribeira da Cruz', directs us southwest (Wp.1 0M) where we climb a few steps and follow a narrow path to pick up the *levada*

.. a water stairway ..

Turning right, our route passes a cairn before heading into the forest where it runs more or less parallel with the ER101.

We soon reach a water stairway (Wp.2 10M) before progressing deeper into this wonderful section of natural forest. We walk through dense sub-tropical vegetation, rocky cliffs and deep ravines where the vegetation is lush and waterfalls plunge into lovely pools formed behind the *levada*.

.. dense subtropical vegetation ..

In places the irrigation channel is carved into the rock face, these damp and humid conditions supporting many species of lichens and mosses. Of particular interest is the abundance of liverwort covering the surrounding rocks and carpeting the pathway under our feet, while the European Chain Fern grows to huge proportions.

This area is also the habitat of the Long-toed Pigeon (Columba Trocaz), one of only two Madeiran endemics - shy creatures who, if disturbed by our footsteps, will escape above the canopy giving us only a glimpse of fluttering wings.

At the head of the gorge

We reach the first of the two largest waterfalls, this one with a good surface underfoot and safety fencing, but expect to get wet after heavy rainfall unless you make a detour across the stream bed below the fall. The second waterfall is reached a few minutes later and is slightly more difficult, the crossing taking us over boulders and stones. There's less chance here of getting wet, but care is needed negotiating this section.

Shortly after leaving the waterfall, a path crosses the *levada* (Wp.3 25M). This emerges through a rustic gate on our left then drops down right to reach the ER101, an alternative exit if the weather is bad.

The final gorge at **Ribeira do Tristão** is dark and damp with a waterfall and pool at the valley head. We negotiate this by crossing the weir and whilst the gorge is deep to our right, the pathway is protected. A few minutes ahead the natural forest diminishes (Wp.4 30M) and is abruptly taken over by an area of Eucalyptus and Pine, much of which has been cleared due to fire damage several years ago. The plus side of this is that we now get good views down to the coast.

Ascending a series of log steps (Wp.5 40M), we leave the *levada* for a short detour before rejoining it.

Montbretia

Along the next section our pathway is adorned with exotic flora; Passion flower from S. America, large yellow Ginger Lily from the Himalayas, Montbretia from S. Africa and European Fuchsia are all found here during the spring and summer months.

Although these large flowering species are a delight to the eye, they are unfortunately extremely invasive and so a threat to Madeira's endemic flora.

Heading back into more indigenous forest, we arrive at the water treatment building of **Reservatória Achadas da Cruz** across from which is a flight of steps on our right (Wp.6 55M), our route down to **Achadas da Cruz**, though for now we ignore the steps and continue beside the *levada*. We pass through a rustic gate, our path veering left, soon crossing a narrow stream. Passing through another gate, we then arrive at a derelict corn mill hidden in the trees. In the past, the *levada* was used to power the grinders of this historic little mill and it passed under the building through a small archway, which is still visible (Wp.7 62M).

The extended route to the source of the *levada* at **Ribeira da Cruz** and down to the start of the PR7 trail on the ER101 would take another 2 hours, but for our shortened circular walk we return to the steps at the water treatment building (Wp.6 70M). Here we have two choices; either to return the same way along the *levada* or to descend the steps to reach the ER101 (Wp.8 75M).

From the bottom of the stairway we can turn left to make an optional detour into the centre of the village where a bar and taxi can be found, while turning right and following the road for 2.5 kilometres (passing another bar) will take us back to the **Santa** forestry post. Following regional roads is not something I would normally recommend, but this reasonably quiet section of the ER101 is lined with agapanthus and hydrangea and passes through a stunning section of the natural forest; it's also a quicker route back to the starting point (Wp.1 120M); there is also another bar/restaurant on the roadside shortly after leaving **Achadas da Cruz**; the choice is yours.

33 LEVADA DA RIBEIRA DA JANELA - LAMACEIROS

The **Ribeira da Janela** gorge which runs from **Rabaçal** down to the north coast is one of the most extensive areas of unspoiled landscape on the island. The *levada* of the same name follows its contours for fifteen kilometres, providing unforgettable views almost every step of the way.

Lamaceiros is the most popular access point, our trail following a six kilometre stretch initially along a well-manicured path lined with agapanthus and hydrangea, before heading deeper into the valley and the natural forest. We negotiate two tunnels en-route (a torch is needed) separated by a spectacular gorge and waterfall. Our final destination is an old *levada* house, an ideal spot for a picnic with magnificent views from the terrace and the company of tame chaffinches eager for titbits.

The attractively landscaped area around the start at **Lamaceiros** water house also offers barbeque buildings, toilets and play areas as well as an adjacent bar/restaurant.

The **Levada da Ribeira da Janela** was closed during 2009 for extensive repair and upgrade but following the floods in February 2010 the channel suffered further damage. The author surveyed the route in April 2010 and whilst repair work was ongoing, found the route to be safe; the works did not in any way detract from the beauty of this walk.

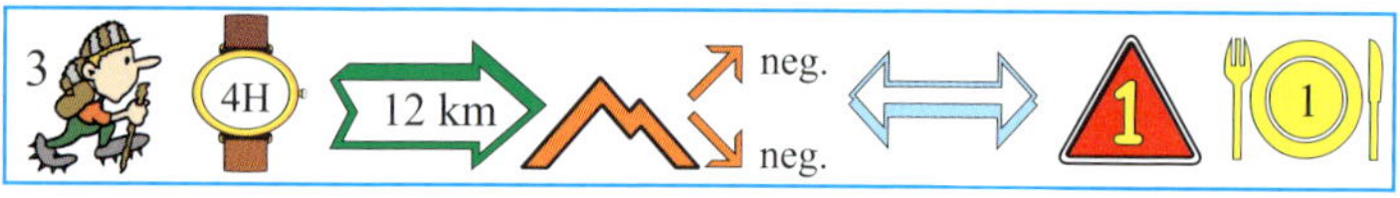

Access by car or taxi:
Leave **Porto Moniz** on the ER101 for the zigzag climb up the escarpment to reach a roundabout. Going left, a new, well-signed section of road continues through the village to the **Lamaceiros** water house. From easterly or southerly areas follow the ER105 over **Paúl da Serra,** turning right onto the ER101. **Lamaceiros** and the *levada* are signed off right a short distance below the junction.

Access by bus:
Alight at **Porto Moniz** and take a taxi to **Levada da Ribeira da Janela**. Taxis are also available from **Lamaceiros** for your return.

We start our walk by picking up the channel beside the water tanks and following it right on a grassy path alongside the rustic fencing.

Crossing over a tarred road, our route is signed (Wp.1 2M) as it heads in and out of the woodland beside flower-filled borders along the well-constructed channel, the pathway wide and good underfoot. Six

The sign at Wp.1

Along the channel shoulder

minutes later we pass the first of three picnic areas strategically placed to take in the magnificent views along this route. We reach the second picnic site a few minutes later (Wp.2 18M) and look down the valley to the riverbed and the **Janela** rock on the coastline.

The natural forest takes over, becoming dark and humid and soon we pass beside a large water run-off (Wp.3 46M). Purple flowering sorrel (Oxalis purpurea) adorns our route as we pass into the denser forest contouring around numerous valley heads.

Oxalis purpurea

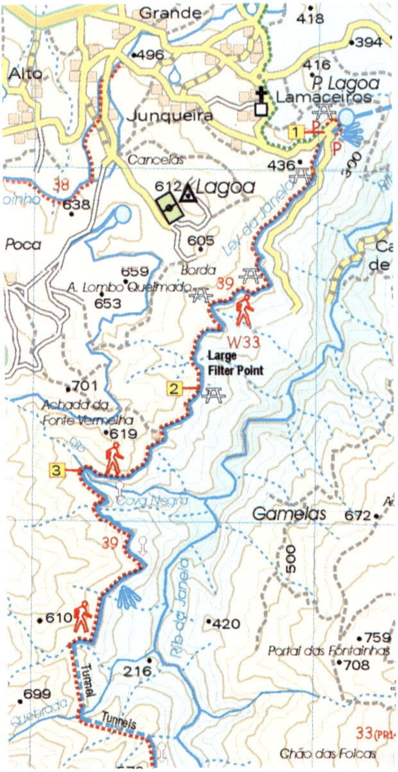

Occasionally small waterfalls spray down the sheer rock walls and here many species of fern and lichens thrive. We arrive at a huge excavated section, part of the recent safety improvements where the channel has been rebuilt and redirected, the remains of the old channel planted with masses of agapanthus.

Rounding a rocky valley head, we arrive at the entrance to the first tunnel (86M), just under 200m long and taking around nine minutes to walk through; the path is quite wet and muddy in places, but it's reasonably good underfoot. Don't forget your torch!

.. we emerge from the tunnel ..

We emerge from the tunnel above a deep gorge where a spectacular waterfall cascades over the *levada* (95M). It's such a beautiful spot and we don't even need to get wet as an amazing tin roof protects us from the flow; there's also safety rustic fencing around the arc of the gorge.

.. a spectacular waterfall ..

A few metres beyond the waterfall, the *levada* enters the second tunnel (100M); this is quite short but curves in the middle, the end only visible from the halfway point. A few metres after exiting, the channel is covered with concrete slabs and the *levada* cut against the rock walls; it's quite precipitous but hand rails are provided for security.

Around fifteen minutes after the tunnel we arrive at an old *levada* water house (120M), a pleasant spot for a rest and to take in the views.

This is the end of the trail and we return by the same route, enjoying the different perspectives on the homeward journey. Once back at the tarred road at **Lamaceiros** (Wp.1 240M) we turn left, passing the car park on our right, to reach the bar/restaurant for some welcome refreshment.

The manicured levada at Lamaceiros

For those wishing to take a taxi back to **Porto Moniz**, a local taxi driver, Jorge Gomez, can be contacted on 291 852 164 or mobile: 966 045 524.

Alternatively, those wishing to walk back to the town should take the **Lamaceiros** road west as far as **Santa** church on the ER101, picking up Walk 30 to descend **Caminho do Pico** on the scenic route into the centre of **Porto Moniz**. (Allow 2hrs - 8kms - descent 460m).

34 LEVADA NOVA - FAJÃ DA OVELHA to PONTA DO PARGO

Since the opening of the VE3, the west of the island has become an extremely popular destination for walkers; eventually, this highway will reach **Ponta do Pargo**. Our walk follows a section of **Levada Nova**, which in total flows 50 km along the south west coast from its source above **Ponta do Sol** to its termination in **Cabo**.

.. lovely views of the coastline ..

The channel, at a height of 640m, crosses open hillsides with lovely views of the coastline along this western section. We negotiate a number of valley heads and dip in and out of woodland and head through agricultural settlements on this tranquil and safe trail. It's an ideal walk for breaking down into shorter sections as it crosses over the ER101 in three places, noted in our text. There's also an optional extension at the end of the trail to include a circular route to the sea cliffs.

Ponta do Pargo, at the far western point of the island, boasts the manned lighthouse of **O Farol** sitting on the sea cliffs with a *miradouro* and **Casa de Chá** close by. It's also an important area for Madeiran birds, where many terrestrial species as well as seabirds, can be spotted.

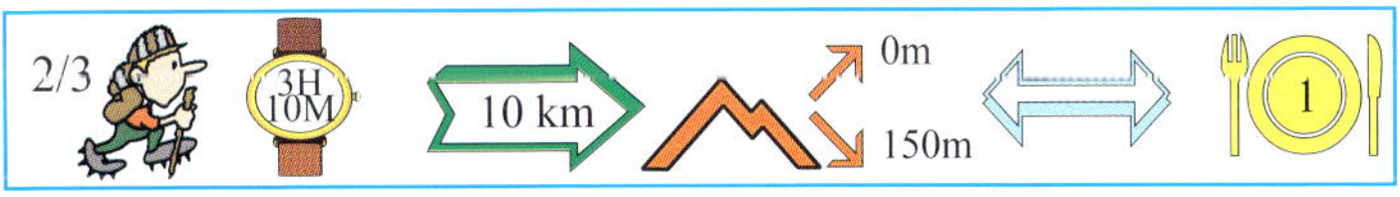

Access by hire car or taxi:
Take the VE3 west toward **Fajã da Ovelha**, continuing on the ER222 before turning left onto the ER223 signed 'Paúl do Mar'. **Levada Nova** crosses over the road 100m below the junction.

Access by bus:
Rodoeste bus routes N°80 between **Funchal** and **Porto Moniz** via **Rapaseira** and N°142 between **Funchal** and **Ponta do Pargo** serve this area.

Leaving the ER223 (Wp.1 0M) we head off right along the channel shoulder, our path swinging right and passing through a stand of pines before continuing beside agricultural plots where superb views of the coast open up. In spring and summer the footpath is flanked with wild flowers; honeysuckle, Madeira crane's-bill, sweet violets, calla lilies and morning glory can be found. Also not to be missed is the frequent appearance of damsel flies,

Levada Nova Fajã da Ovelha

Monarch butterflies (Danaus plexippus) and the Clouded Yellow (Colias crocea) flitting between the plants. In the cooler weather, the Migratory Locust (Locusta migratoria) can also be seen. Along most of the trail the *levada* is flanked by bracken, bramble and gorse; we are soon aware of Madeira Wall Lizards scurrying into the undergrowth.

Madeiran Wall Lizard

Arriving at the hamlet of **São Lourenço** (Wp.2 15M), we cross over a narrow lane dotted with A-framed barns to pick up the channel on the opposite side. Now heading in a northerly direction and around a valley head, there's evidence of the highway development encroaching this area (in Aug 2011) and although the *levada* will be protected, there is likely to be some change in the near future.

Colina da Fajã hotel

A few minutes later we arrive in **Sitio de São João** beside the pretty **Colina da Fajã** hotel (Wp.3 30M), a strikingly designed building with a wonderful olive tree in the front garden.

At this point the *levada* is culverted so we pick it up again around 15 metres ahead on the left of the concrete lane. Two minutes after crossing another narrow lane beside a pretty pink house, we head out along the open hillside, at this elevation enjoying increasingly lovely views down to the sea. The channel soon turns right and below us on our left, is **Rua das Eirinhas**, the second main road leading into **Fajã**. A few minutes later we reach the ER101 regional road, completing the first section of the trail (Wp.4 45M).

Crossing over, our path is now elevated above the road as it follows the contours; here again is evidence of the new highway development where tunnel entrances have appeared on either side of the valley (in Aug 2011). Nevertheless this doesn't spoil our enjoyment as we head into the **Ribeira dos Marinheiros** valley. It's really pretty along this section with rocky walls, rivulets and lush vegetation. Soon we hear the sound of rushing water as the river below us cascades over its stony bed. At the valley head, we cross on a stepped bridge (Wp.5 55M) with waterfalls and pools to our right, then head out of the valley back towards the regional road.

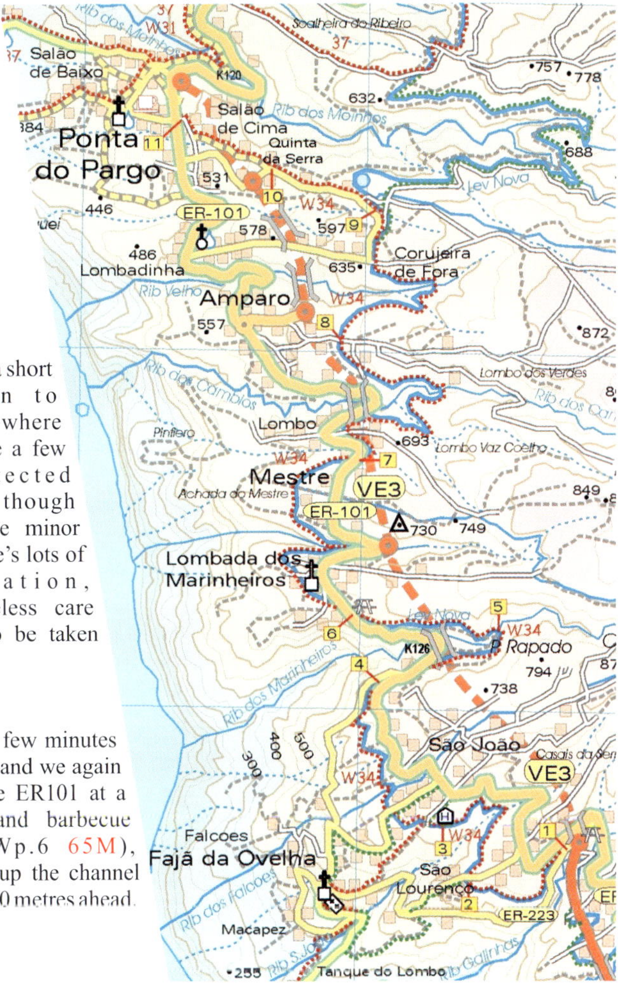

There's a short section to follow where there are a few unprotected drops; though these are minor and there's lots of vegetation, nevertheless care needs to be taken here.

Another few minutes walking and we again cross the ER101 at a picnic and barbecue site (Wp.6 65M), picking up the channel around 10 metres ahead.

Our route leads us through the settlement of **Lombo dos Marinheiros**, crossing cultivated fields, agricultural terraces and orchards before traversing around a number of valley heads where lush vegetation and mixed woodland take over; here we find Sweet Chestnut, Oak, Maple, Walnut, Acacia and Laurels.

Along the next stretch of open hillside we have clear views of the lighthouse and the radio mast on **Pico das Favas** at **Ponta da Pargo** and with the village of **Amparo** ahead of us, our pathway swings right to arrive for the third time on the ER101, concluding the second section of the walk (Wp.7 105M).

Crossing over the road, the channel loops behind a newly created picnic area where picnic tables, barbecue facilities and toilets can be found. Following the *levada* from the picnic site, our route heads through a small hamlet with apple orchards and orange groves. Beside the first house, the *levada* is slabbed

.. orange groves ..

over but a number of gaps make our progress tricky; it's possible however to detour around the house by descending and ascending steps on either side. The trail now leads into an agricultural area before arriving at a valley head amongst abundant eucalyptus where we cross a pretty river by means of a weir.

We head out of the valley through a stand of pines before the sound of rushing water heralds our arrival at a second valley head; after crossing a track, we reach a beautiful spot with another river tumbling over waterfalls. Here we climb a few steps to cross over the weir before descending to the opposite bank. Approaching another farming community, again with lots of A-framed barns, we cross over a road above **Amparo** (Wp.8 155M). After another few minutes walking, as more houses appear, our path runs parallel with a tarred road. A few metres ahead we arrive at a concrete driveway and leave the *levada* to drop onto the road (Wp.9 170M). (Note: The irrigation channel continues from here for another 8 kms to its end in **Cabo**, a parish of **Ponta do Pargo**. This takes over 2 hours to walk with a descent of 180 m to the chapel and headland).

Turning right along the road, we head down towards **Ponta do Pargo**. Around 700 metres ahead, we take a right fork signed 'Rua Salão de Cima' (Wp.10). On reaching a *fonte* we follow the road right and then left, to end in the village centre (Wp.11 190M), a total of 1.2kms from the *levada* with a descent of 150m; taxis and buses are available to return to our start.

Extension

At the end of this walk an extension can be added, visiting **O Farol**, the *miradouro* and **Casa de Chá** restaurant. Both are situated on the headland below the village. The landscape around the lighthouse is wild, open grassland, the coastline is magnificent and in spring the wild flowers are a delight. Allow around one hour for this 4 km extension with an additional descent and ascent of 170m.

The road network for the new golf course in **Ponta do Pargo** is currently being developed (June 2011). As a result, the lane from the village down to **Pico das Favas** is closed. Therefore access to the lighthouse, **Casa de Chá** and the headland is via the church where you follow the signs for 'O Farol and Miradouro'.

Casa de Chá

35 FAJÃ DA OVELHA to PAÚL DO MAR

There was a time before the creation of the regional roads when **Paúl do Mar** was only accessible by boat or along the rugged cliff paths linking the village to trade and amenities in other settlements. We follow one of these ancient cobbled pathways, except for short sections where the route have been obliterated by development where we follow a short stretch of road to link the pathway in **Fajã**. Starting at an elevation of 600m and dropping to sea level, this safe trail has a reasonably easy descent due to the number of zigzags which ease the overall gradient significantly.

Paúl do Mar harbour

The views from the cliffs are wonderful; once down, you'll feel the buzz of this lovely traditional fishing village nestled in its stunning position beneath the cliffs. There are a number of bars and restaurants and a wander through the enchanting narrow streets leading to the harbour is a must. Also impressive is the bronze statue erected on a rocks looking out to sea, erected as a tribute to fishermen past and present.

The bronze statue

Access by car or taxi:
Refer to Walk 34 for directions to the starting point.

Access by bus:
Rodoeste bus routes N°80 between **Funchal** and **Porto Moniz** via **Fajã da Ovelha**, and N°142 between **Funchal** and **Ponta do Pargo**, serve this area.

At first, we follow the same route as Walk 34 (Wp.1 to Wp.3 30M) along **Levada Nova** for 30 minutes until we reach the **Colina da Fajã Hotel** in **Sitio de São João**. Once at this charming hotel and hamlet, we leave the *levada* to take a concrete drive on the left of the courtyard, signed 'Vereda da Soalheita'. Dropping down steps facing an old cottage, the route veers right as our descent on the ancient cobbled trail to **Paúl do Mar** begins. Soon crossing a driveway and passing a barn on our left, we reach a thicket of trees on our right; as our path becomes steeper and uneven, the church and steeple come into view.

Meeting a T-junction of paths with the area in front fenced, we turn right and then immediately left, to drop down beside the fenced land. A few metres

Passiflora actinia

ahead, look out for the wonderful scented Passiflora actinia as we descend a quaint narrow pathway between houses and gardens to arrive again on the ER223 (Wp.4 48M).

Crossing the road, we head towards the church of **Fajã**, a lovely building of Moorish influence with huge date palms in the grounds. At the main gates we descend steps and turn left, then right to enter the walled cemetery. A gate on the right leads out beside the tennis courts to a pathway, which rejoins the ER223 (Wp.5 50M). Our trail follows the road left for a short distance before taking a right turn just beyond a bend, signed 'Rua Dr. Mário Correia Sardinha' (Wp.6 55M).

the Antigo Fio

We reach the area of **Macapez** where we pick up a path on the left with a ceramic sign indicating 'Antigo Fio da Fajã da Ovelha' (Wp.7 70M), approximately 800m in total from the church.

Following the cobbled path, we descend to a stone bridge over the **Ribeira São João** and climb the opposite bank where the path peaks on the cliff tops. **Paúl do Mar** is now in view and we begin our main descent. Passing between two derelict cottages, we arrive at the **Antigo Fio**, a cable lift used to transport produce between **Paúl** and **Fajã**, sitting on a platform on the cliff tops.

Looking down on Paúl do Mar from Wp.8

Remnants of the old cable lift, wheel and buildings still remain in this attractive area surrounded by rustic fencing, which is also a superb lookout point (Wp.8 80M).)

Another interesting feature of this area is the dominance of Agave Americana or Century Plant (referring to the long time the plant takes to flower). This South American tropical species, introduced to Europe in the 17th century, is now widely cultivated. With its large basal rosette of fibrous blue-green sword shaped leaves (as shown in our photo, above) and yellow flowers which grow into tall trees, it's quite remarkable.

Descending the cobbled path

From here on, our route becomes quite steep as it zigzags down the cliffs, passing beside ochre coloured volcanic rock along much of its descent. We reach a cave on our left (Wp.9 90M) and the further we drop, views of the hairpin bends and tunnels carved through rock of one of the island's most spectacular roads appear dramatically.

Vegetation along the cliffs includes Globularia, Prickly Pear, Pride of Madeira and Houseleeks; also look out for the rare wild olive trees, a Madeiran endemic that grows on the precarious slopes of these cliffs.

Approaching sea level, the vegetation changes; bananas and other crops appear as the trail passes through the hamlet of **Ribeira das Galinhas**. A few metres after crossing the bridge (Wp.10 105M) we arrive on **Avenida dos Pescadores Paúlenses**, the **Paúl do Mar** promenade.

Soon passing **Bar Poleiro** on our left - a convivial place to stop for a drink (Wp.11 110M) - we head along the sea front to the area of **Igreja**. As the road bends left (Wp.12 125M), our route continues straight ahead through charming narrow streets, to arrive at the harbour (Wp.13 135M).

36 PRAZERES to JARDIM DO MAR

A spectacular and exhilarating walk along an ancient pathway connecting **Prazeres** with the coastal village of **Jardim do Mar**, this was one of the main access routes to the village before roads arrived in the 1960s. It has recently been designated as the official **PR20 Vereda do Jardim do Mar** walking route.

Looking along the coast from Prazeres

The trail begins at the **Jardim Atlántico Hotel** in **Lombo da Rocha** situated on the beautiful headland overlooking the cliffs and coastline. This is also the starting point for the **PR19** route **Caminho Real do Paúl do Mar**, which drops down the cliffs to the harbour in **Paúl**.

The villages are vastly different; **Jardim do Mar** is a quieter agricultural village with a tradition of wine making**,** while **Paúl do Mar** is predominantly associated with fishing. Both routes are strenuous and demanding with descents of around 550m along very steep gradients, but they are stunning and there are no sheer drops on either of the pathways.

The two routes can be joined to make a circular by taking the road tunnel or the rocky coastal path to join the villages. But caution is needed for this latter option, as access along the beach is not possible during the winter months or at high tide.

Walking poles, good footwear, long trousers, hat and sun cream are recommended for both these routes; also remember to take lots of water.

Circular Option
The information bar (above) shows the ratings for the linear route. Ratings for the circular option are: 5 walker, 4 hours, 10km, ascents & descents 550 metres

Access by car or taxi:
Follow the VE3 from **Ribeira Brava** to **Prazeres Village**. The walk's start at the **Jardim Atlántico Hotel** in **Lombo da Rocha** is well signposted from the village centre. Parking is available either in the hotel grounds or in the overspill car park.

Access by bus:
The Rodoeste bus N°142 from **Funchal** to **Ponta do Pargo** serves this area. Alight at **Prazeres** village. As there is no regular bus service from **Jardim do Mar** to **Prazeres**, a taxi or walking are the options for the return journey back to the starting point.

From the hotel gardens (Wp.1 0M) we head up the access road passing bar/restaurant **Vista Prazeres** on our right and a few metres ahead turn right (Wp.2 5M) crossing over the expresso bridge to continue along the country lane. A short distance ahead we reach a cobbled lane on the right signed 'miradouro' (Wp.3 15M), which descends between two attractive houses and is our route to the headland. The lane steeply descends, passing beside stands of pine and oak with another large estate to our right. We pass through dappled sunlight, accompanied by the sound of twittering birds. The lane ends at two houses on the cliff tops where a cobbled path drops between the houses to take us to the *miradouro* (Wp.4 20M).

Our route leaves the *miradouro*, dropping below one of the house gardens winding down between the vegetation and here we can look down on **Paúl do Mar** harbour. Tall grasses overhang the path as the trail continues, at first down a reasonable gradient, getting significantly steeper as we progress. It's a rugged, long descent, in places overgrown and rocky and can be extremely wet, so care is needed. However, the path is well defined with rustic fencing on a few selected sections and the views are splendid with **Jardim do Mar** getting closer and closer as we descend.

Around fifty minutes from the cliff-top *miradouro* we arrive at the **Jardim do Mar Miradouro** and barbeque area approximately 100 m above the village (Wp.5 73M). This long, flat ledge offers panoramic views over the village and is protected with rustic fencing. There's a stone barbeque, table, rustic seating and water tap so it's a good place to stop for a rest and picnic before our final descent into the village.

A loaded grape vine

The trail continues on stone and concrete steps leading down between the dry stone walling of the agricultural plots where figs and vegetables abound, then passes beside small vineyards and banana

Banana crops

plantations which continue throughout the village.

Moinho, the old mill

A narrow *levada* rushes down beside us as we approach the village, the first proper building being the beautifully restored water-powered corn mill of **Moinho** on our left, just before the first houses (Wp.6 81M). Its mechanisms are powered by the *levada*, which enters the mill at the rear of the building.

The coastal path to Paúl do Mar

Now dropping down a mosaic pathway between the houses and pretty gardens, we reach a T-junction of paths (Wp.7 83M), turning right in the direction of **Paúl do Mar**. The path continues to descend between more properties, finally reaching the promenade and pebbly beach.

Note: The latter is the route of the coastal path across to **Paúl do Mar**, but first we take time to see **Jardim do Mar**. Those wishing to cross the coastal path should seek advice from local people as to its current status before venturing across the beach.

Turning left along the promenade, we circle the village to arrive at the **Portinha Bar** (Wp.8 95M), constructed from a small house; there's also a swimming area beside the jetty. From the bar we retrace our steps for around 25 metres, ignoring the wide vehicle access road and instead taking the

The village square

narrow mosaic lane beside the cemetery leading to the village church, square and hotel.

The remainder of the village is pedestrianised with narrow mosaic passageways leading off the square.

Following the 'Vereda da Igreja' sign (Wp.9 105M) will lead us to the very popular **Joe's Bar** with its pretty beer garden. The ambience is brilliant and the food good quality and reasonably priced. There's also a small art and craft gallery just before the bar that's well worth a visit (open Sept - April).

Along the mosaic path to Joe's Bar

Those not wishing to continue on to **Paúl do Mar** have two options for getting back to **Prazeres** by either returning by the same route or by taking a taxi back to the starting point. A taxi can be arranged at the hotel or call Juca 96 60 38 547 or the Paúl do Mar taxi 96 30 75 612

Alternative route descending to Paúl do Mar (1.8 kms - allow 1hr 15mins)
This route begins at the bottom of the hotel driveway where a finger post directs you left signed 'Paúl do Mar PR19'. Passing between the gardens and buildings we descend the path with stunning views to the right, before dropping down between the apartment blocks to the start of the trail on the cliff tops.

Originally the municipal path to **Paúl do Mar**, it has recently been repaved and protective fencing added. The trail makes a steep zigzag descent contouring around the cliffs, finally reaching the lovely harbour and village with its shady bars and narrow streets.

37 LEVADA NOVA - PRAZERES to ESTRELA DA CALHETA

Bordered by the **Parque Natural da Madeira** and set against a spectacular backdrop of forest and mountains, the picturesque parish of **Prazeres** is an extremely popular destination for walkers. The village has lots to offer, with its lovely twin-spired church and adjacent *pedagógica* and *casa de chá*.

There's a parish zoo with a beautiful herb garden, tea house, small art gallery and cider bar; the menagerie includes Emu, Llama, Bambi and miniature ponies as well as many unusual species of swine and waterfowl while the tea house offers a wide selection of herbal teas, preserves, cider and plants. Lower down the village a Farmers' Sunday Market takes place where freshly harvested vegetables, fruit and flowers, as well as freshly baked bread, cakes and handicrafts are on offer. A choice of bars and restaurants can be found around the church.

Our route along this section of **Levada Nova** as far as **Calheta** has recently been restored, providing a safe walk with no precipitous places. It's also a good choice for hot sunny days as most of the route passes through shady forest as it winds alongside the mountain slopes.

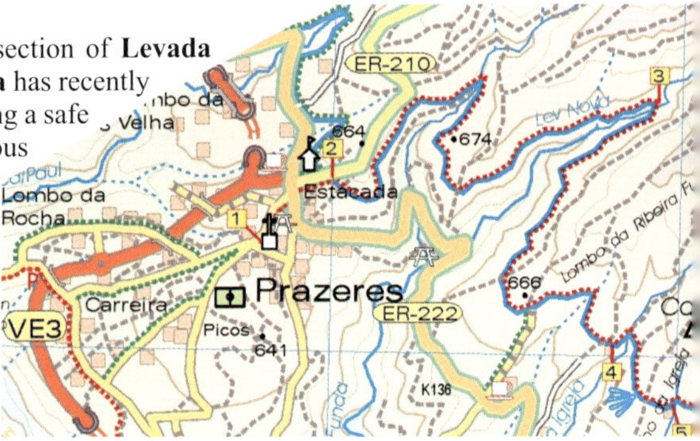

There are several rivers and streams en route, one particularly picturesque with waterfalls, crystal clear pools and stepping stones, where you can enjoy a rest or picnic in an ideal setting. The final 350 metre descent into the centre of **Estrela da Calheta** can be tiring and tough on the knees; however, it's optional. If preferred, you can arrange for a taxi to collect you where the *levada* crosses the ER211.

Access by hire car or taxi:
Follow the VE3 from **Ribeira Brava** to the village of **Prazeres**; roadside parking can be found close to the church.

Access by bus:
Rodoeste Bus N°142 from **Funchal** to **Ponta do Pargo** serves this area. Alight at **Prazeres** village. Return from **Calheta** - Bus N°s 80,107,115,142.

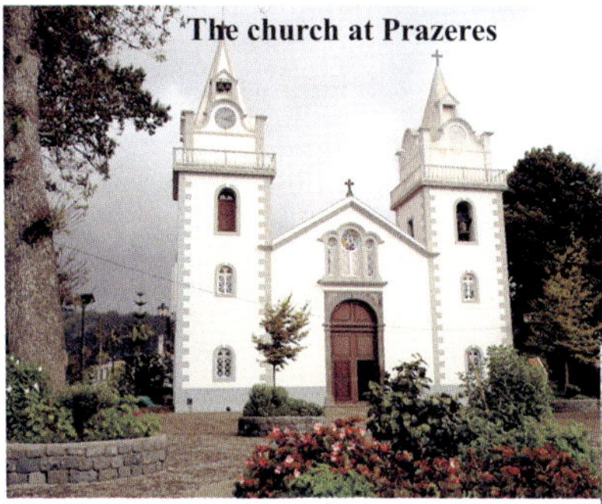
The church at Prazeres

From the village centre (Wp.1 0M) we head towards the crossroad and continue on the ER210 signed 'Fonte do Bispo'. The *levada* crosses the road close to the *Posto Florestal*, approximately 100 metres above the junction and our trail begins on the right following the channel upstream (Wp.2 5M). After passing beside a new housing development we immediately enter the forest, leaving the village behind. At first dominated by pine and eucalyptus, other species soon appear including a few stray apple trees.

Agapanthus line our path

Our path is lined with Lily of the Nile (Agapanthus) and Hydrangea, the conditions clearly perfect for these stunning blue flowering plants; during the summer months you'll rarely see a more splendid display. As the *levada* flows deeper into the forest, looping around the mountain ridges, views of the coastline can be seen from a number of clearings. Soon we reach **Ribeira Funda** (Wp.3 45M) where rocky pools flow into a weir beside the channel shoulder.

Thirty minutes later we arrive at the **Atalhinho Water House** (Wp.4 75M). At this point a road drops down to the right passing the **Atrio Estalagem** (Guest House) before joining the ER222 in **Estreito**, making this an alternative option for anyone wanting to shorten the route; however, the further we continue on from the **Atalhinho Water House**, the more picturesque our route becomes. Meandering once again through the forest, our route is adorned with wild fuchsia.

fine views of Paúl da Serra from Levada Nova

The channel passes between a disused farm house and orchard (Wp.5) and minutes later beside a fertile grazing area (Wp.6). Soon after the scenery opens up, giving us splendid views of the **Paúl da Serra** slopes, the valley to our right now extremely deep; the tops of the eucalyptus trees growing on the slopes are almost at eye level.

.. stepping stones guide us across ..

A little over two hours walking brings us to **Ribeira da Achada** (Wp.7 140M), where the river is hemmed in by craggy mountain slopes covered in bracken and heaths, in autumn turning to hues of red, gold and brown. Stepping stones guide us across the weir, though first be sure to take a rest beside the lovely clear pool.

Our final stretch of the *levada* route takes us around two isolated valleys high above **Estrela da Calheta** where Laurel, Oak, Sweet Chestnut and Mimosa dominate the forest. Eventually, after passing beside a small reservoir, the channel becomes paved; after a small water house on our left, we arrive in **Lombo do Salão** on the ER211 regional road leading down from **Rabaçal** to **Calheta** (Wp.8 200M).

Turning right, we leave the *levada* to follow the road on a steep descent through areas of woodland and farming land, passing beside orchards, orange groves and traditional agricultural houses. As newer houses start to appear, we reach a junction turning right onto a much newer and wider road leading down the valley (Wp.9). A further descent brings us to another junction at the *Centro do Saúde* (Calheta Hospital) (Wp.10) and going straight ahead, we make a final short climb into the centre of **Estrela** where taxis, buses and bars can be found (Wp.11 240M).

38 LEVADA NOVA - LORETO to CANHAS

Valerian along the Levada Nova

This trail follows an eight kilometre stretch of **Levada Nova** as it flows through spectacular scenery, enhanced by a profusion of wild flowers. The first of two walks starting from this point, it follows the *levada* to its junction with the ER 209 above **Canhas** before continuing along the regional road into the village centre.

The second walk leaves the channel just before the hamlet of **Pomar** making a gradual descent to **Achada de Santo Antão** followed by a much steeper gradient down to sea level at **Madalena do Mar**.

The aqueduct between these two parishes has only recently reopened (April 2011) following extensive restoration work. The *levada* has been rebuilt along most of its length and substantial safety fencing has been erected on all precipitous sections, now making this a safe and almost vertigo-free trail.

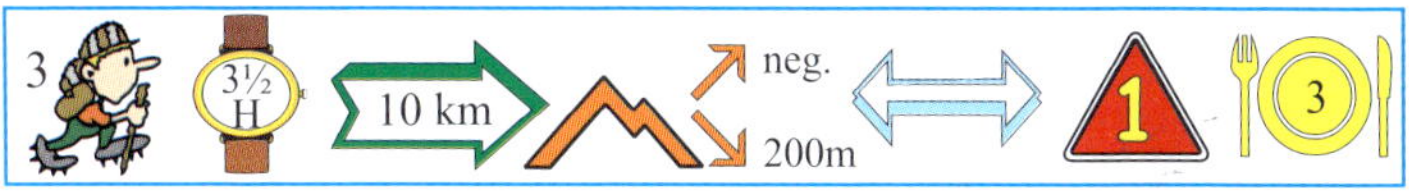

Access by hire car or taxi:
Take the ER 222 west from **Loreto** village taking the first right, signed 'Paúl da Serra'. Follow the road for 1.3 km to where the *levada* crosses the road passing between two water tanks and a small industrial estate.

Access by bus:
Rodoeste offer a limited service to **Calheta** and **Canhas**; bus Nºs 115 &142.

Leaving the road (Wp.1 0M), we follow the *levada* in an easterly direction skirting below the southern edge of the pine and eucalyptus forest.

Arco da Calheta

Within a few minutes we take in wonderful views over the coastline and the depression of **Arco da Calheta**. The spring flora cannot fail to impress; Wild Valerian in shades of red, pink and white cover the slopes on either side of the channel and there's blue and yellow vetch, purple and pink bindweed, yellow flowering broom and orange and yellow nasturtiums - spectacular!

Ten minutes along, we pass beside a small water house and water regulation point (Wp.2 12M) before crossing over a cobbled track leading up to **Pinheiro** village higher up the ridge (Wp.3 15M). In another ten minutes the

channel becomes paved (Wp.4 25M) before narrowing significantly where it is cut into the rock face. Originally a dangerous section, this has now been protected with sturdy metal posts and wire, making it safe for walkers.

.. an attractive tiny pond ..

As the path widens (Wp.5 40M) we return to more leisurely walking and five minutes after crossing over a forest track (Wp.6 43M), the trail reaches a short tunnel (Wp.7 48M) - no torch needed. On emerging we find ourselves at an attractive tiny pond beside the channel. From this point on the *levada* flows between the rock face and deep-forested slopes, the damp conditions providing an ideal habitat for many water-loving plants. Of particular interest is the endemic disc houseleek (aeonium glandulosum), a plant with a single leaf rosette growing in the basalt crevices and clinging to the rock face which changes colour from green to pink during summer.

aeonium glandulosum

Now sweeping into the forested valley of **Ribeira da Madalena**, the hamlets of **Pomar** and **Pinheiro** come into view, set against a backdrop of the **Paúl da Serra** hills. Here a track appears, descending sharp right into the valley below

(Wp.8 60M); this is the route for Walk 39 leading down to **Achada de Santo Antão** in **Arco**.

The detour over the bridge

Ignoring this and continuing for a few more minutes, a small waterfall and water run-off come into view, here we make a detour down a narrow earthen path to the right, crossing a bridge over the **Ribeira do Pico da Urze** before climbing the opposite banking to rejoin the channel. If you miss this path and find yourself rounding the valley head on a very narrow section, you should return at once and locate the path.

The forest thins out as we approach **Sitio do Pomar** (Wp.9 75M). This tiny hamlet was inhabited until quite recently; it's not difficult to imagine what life must have been like here before the access road was created to **Pinheiro** village above; the track we passed a few minutes earlier was the original route to civilization and amenities.

banana maracujá passion flower

Leaving **Pomar**, our trail veers left towards the valley head passing beside fig and walnut trees, the latter hosting the pretty, though invasive, banana maracujá passion flower. Crossing a newly constructed bridge over the **Ribeira da Madalena** gorge (Wp.10 80M) protected with safety fencing, our route heads out of the valley, passing a few narrow sections before a long stretch where the channel is culverted.

From this point the forest begins to thin out and we have fine views south to **Madalena** and back to the hamlets where the waterfall of **Ribeira do Pico da Urze** can been seen crashing into the valley. Soon turning east, our trail leads out of the forest (Wp.11 100M) into an agricultural area and after passing beside a nursery on our left, crosses over a tarred road at **Eiras** (Wp.12 110M). We pick up the *levada* again at the top of a driveway on the opposite side of the road.

The final section leads us through inhabited agricultural areas crossing a number of concrete access roads and another small river. Still dipping in and out of the forest, now pine and eucalyptus, our trail arrives at **Barreiro** on the ER209, the regional road leading down from **Paúl da Serra** to **Canhas** (Wp.13 170M). Turning right and following the road for half a kilometer brings us to a crossroad beside the **Levada do Poiso** clock tower (Wp.14 180M). A taxi can be arranged from one of the three bars situated around the junction or alternatively we can walk for another 1.5 km down the road into the centre of **Canhas** where taxis and buses are available. (Wp.15 210M).

39 LORETO to MADALENA DO MAR

A stunning section of *levada*, a short tunnel, a wonderful forest trail, an ancient pathway, banana plantations, charming hamlets and a perfect end beside the sea, make this a spectacular route.

The second of two walks starting from **Loreto**, this trail follows **Levada Nova** for one hour before making a gradual descent through the forest to **Achada de Santo Antão** in **Arco**, then continuing on a much steeper gradient to reach the coast at **Madalena do Mar**. It's a steep down hill (poles are definitely recommended), though it's a small price to pay for such a varied and interesting walk

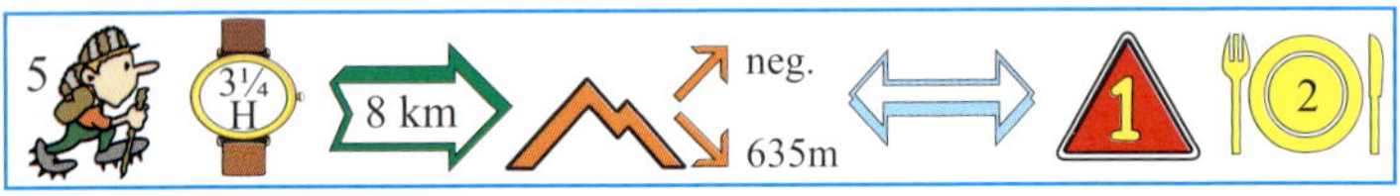

Access by hire car or taxi:
Follow the directions given in Walk 38 to the start of this trail.

Along Levada Nova

Leaving **Loreto**, we follow the directions given for Walk 38 from (Wp.1 to Wp.8 - 60M)**.** This is where we leave the *levada*, going sharp right down the wide and sandy track to descend into the deep-forested valley. This was the original access to the isolated hamlets of **Pomar** and **Pinheiro**; thankfully a road a little higher up the hillside now serves these communities.

Eucalyptus, pines and acacia are the dominant trees, although laurels and holly can also be found. The path through the forest is not steep and there are a few well constructed log stairways.

As the path levels out, we pass beside a huge wall of ochre coloured rock overhanging the path and a few minutes later arrive at a well and an old farm building in **Lombo da Achada** (Wp.9 90M). At the first house on the right, the lane becomes tarred and passing two ponds on our right (Wp.10), throbbing with croaking frogs in springtime, we pass more new property on either side of the lane as it now becomes quite steep, dropping down the ridge to **Achada de Santo Antão**.

We are following **Vereda do Fontanario**; after passing two very large semi-detached houses on our right, we find a slope and steps on our left (Wp.11 95M), which we descend in a southerly direction towards the headland.

Our path zigzags down, soon giving us fantastic views across the valley to where the ER222 snakes down from **Canhas**. We reach a small water station (Wp.12 105M) and the path divides, ignoring the left path we keep straight ahead alongside a narrow water channel. It's quite stony underfoot, so we need to take care although there are no steep drops to worry us.

The road from Canhas

A few minutes later our trail emerges onto the ER222 at **Molados** (Wp.13 115M). Going left ,we walk down the road passing **Bar la Fronteira** on our right. Another 200 metres ahead, we leave the road turning sharp right down concrete steps (Wp.14 125M) onto **Vereda do Barreiro**, a narrow path with street lights and telegraph poles.

From hereon our route is mostly stepped, passing at first through wilder vegetation of prickly pear, fish stunning spurge and giant reeds, before dropping between the banana plantations. At a T-junction with another path we go right down steps, soon emerging onto the regional road (Wp.15 142M); this last section of footpath is signed 'Vereda da Ribeira do Madalena'.

The house at Wp.17

Turning right, we descend the road for a short distance and at a sharp U-bend, steps with green metal handrails descend on the right (Wp.16 160M). This is our route leading through the banana plantations. We arrive at a house (Wp.17) with a well and a pretty passageway to the right; here we go left on another steep stepped descent. Walking poles are definitely helpful on this section to avoid pressure on the knees, but let's not dwell on this slight discomfort; there's plenty to take our interest as we pass between the plantations and the old and new houses.

We soon meet the road again and go right for around 100 metres to another U-bend where we go right down more concrete steps, signed 'Calçada da Palmeira' (Wp.18 170M). The new expresso tunnel entrance and road construction is now directly to our left (April 2011).

Banda de Alem

A little further along we reach the side road of **Rua das Covas** which ends at some bollards around 40 metres ahead (Wp.19 180M). The road, **Banda de Alem**, then becomes concrete as it drops down to a picturesque hamlet where tiny cottages are built into the rock face. It's quite amazing and very quaint with pretty gardens and flower tubs.

Arriving at Madalena

At the bottom of the hill our route turns right, continuing between more attractive properties before coming to an end on the regional road in **Madalena** (Wp.20 190M). Here we cross over and head down a path to the promenade where two bars and a restaurant can be found; we can now partake of a well deserved rest and a cold refreshing drink after our efforts (Wp.21 194M).

40 LOMBADA DA PONTA DO SOL - LEVADA NOVA & LEVADA DO MOINHO

Solar dos Esmeraldos Mansion House

Here's a great day out for anyone who enjoys the natural and built environment, especially if you can't resist a slightly more challenging walk. **Lombada do Ponta do Sol** lies on a mountain ridge at 320 m above sea level. The walk starts at the ancient **Solar dos Esmeraldos** mansion house and **Espirito Santo Chapel**, both of which are worth a visit in their own right.

Espirito Santo Chapel

But this is also an outstanding *levada* walk heading deep into the valley, the lush and diverse flora embellishing the magnificent landscape. The two channels run parallel along the valley side, **Levada do Moinho** starting from behind the chapel, with **Levada Nova** picked up 80 metres above at the hamlet of **Jangão**.

The section of the trail along **Levada Nova** is quite challenging and the drops are sheer, but it's a beautiful route for sure-footed walkers with a head for heights. The precipitous sections start quite soon along the route and are likely to disturb vertigo sufferers; nevertheless, over the last year the *levada* has undergone significant reinstatement. It's also evident that safety railings will be erected in the future but at the time of our survey (May 2011) these were still not in place, so great care is needed walking along this *levada*.

N.B. Due to the terrain along all this route, GPS signals are unreliable. For this reason we include Wp.1 only to get you to the start of the walk.

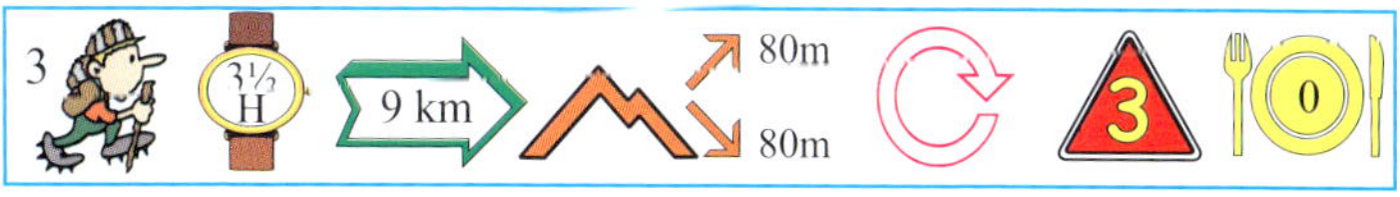

Access by car or taxi:
Follow the VE3 to **Ponta do Sol** Shopping Centre and take the first right up hill to a T-junction where the road meets the ER222. Turn right following the road east for 1km, going left at a sign for 'Lombada da Ponta do Sol'. The road twists and climbs for just over 1km, passing snack bar **La Babaria** on the left. Our destination of **Solar dos Esmeraldos** mansion house and **Espirito Santo Chapel** can be seen above. A little further along take a sharp left to lead into the square beside the chapel.

Access by bus:
Rodoeste buses N°s 4, 8 107,115 pass through **Ponta do Sol** but there is a very limited service to **Lombada**.

From the square (Wp.1 0M), we double back along the road for approximately 100 metres, taking a left turn to climb the tarred road to the hamlet of **Jangão**. After the road bends right we meet a T-Junction and going left here, we pick up the channel a few metres ahead where it crosses over the road (20M).

Following the channel upstream, we leave the hamlet behind, passing small sugar plantations and agricultural terraces and soon views of the distant mountain range towards **Cascalho** and **Bica da Cana** on **Paúl da Serra**, loom before us.

The water channel clings to the valley side and in places is carved into the rock face often with overhangs, where water trickles down into the channel. We pass in and out of a number of side valleys and, at around the mid point, look down to the new industrial area above **Ponta do Sol** (45M).

There are some stunning plants en route, with endemics such as Disc House-Leek (Aeonium glandulosum) and Shrubby Sow Thistle (Sonchus fruiticsus) thriving.

Shortly we arrive at a tunnel entrance - the headroom is quite low at first, but it's dry underfoot and we can see the other end as we enter; remember to take a torch along.

Emerging from the tunnel

As we emerge from the tunnel we find the most exciting part of the trail, as we come face to face with a spectacular waterfall crashing down a rocky chasm into the valley below.

We pass around this large, cavernous gorge the path now leading us behind the waterfall; though it's not difficult or dangerous, care is needed around this section. The path then continues along the opposite side heading out of the valley and here we look down onto a canopy of Willows and Poplars. A few minutes along, we pass a track descending the hillside on our left which will be our route down to **Levada do Moinho**. First though, we continue along the channel to the riverbed and source of **Levada Nova** (100M). There's a wide weir across the river and new sluice gates and channels have been constructed. It's a wonderful spot for a picnic before continuing on our way.

On our return to the track, we pass over a water change point before descending the path to meet **Levada do Moinho**. This is quite steep and also a little slippery, so walking poles are extremely helpful here.

As we arrive on the *levada* (125M) we notice the change in vegetation, now much more lush and humid at this slightly lower elevation (320m).

Lush vegetation as we reach the *levada*

Levada do Moinho

Going left, we round the side valley coming below the waterfall and gorge to cross the river under willows (140M).

This channel, not as precipitous as the higher *levada*, was completely reinstated a few years ago with safety fencing erected along most of its length. It makes for a reasonably easy return to our starting point but there are now a few eroded sections along the shoulder and a number of areas where the safety fencing has been broken, but all is passable with care.

Ten minutes from the waterfall we reach a section where the channel is carved into a high rocky wall which is covered in ferns and lichen and where riverlets spray down on us as we pass along, so expect to get a little wet here. Now winding in and out of small valleys the chapel comes into view as we head back to **Solar dos Esmeraldos**, our path eventually taking us around the back of the chapel and into the square (Wp.1 200M).

In the past, the aqueduct **Moinho** fed a sugar cane mill and the grinding wheel of a corn mill from which it takes its name (*moinho* meaning mill). The latter still stands, close to the chapel and has been restored within a lovely little garden. The chute which directed the water into the mill still exists and it's possible to climb a short flight of steps to peer down inside.

The Solar dos Esmeraldos Estate

The manor house of **Solar dos Esmeraldos**, painted in the traditional rose colour, is now looking very tired, but it's underlying character and elegance is unmistakable. Built by Joaõ Esmeraldo over 500 years ago, this Flemish merchant was the first sugar baron to settle in Madeira and was reputed to be a friend of Christopher Columbus.

Restored mill, Solar dos Esmeraldos

His main residence, Columbus's House in **Funchal**, was demolished in 1876, but the **Museu do Açúcar** in **Praça de Colombo**, provides good documentation for anyone interested in the history of these buildings.

Over the years the house has been extensively modified and is now used as the village school; in the intervening years, it was also used as a convent. The **Espirito Santo Chapel**, rebuilt in the 18th century, is a lovely example of Portuguese religious architecture. Its interior is extremely ornate with rich baroque carvings and there are many wonderful *azulejos* (traditional blue and white glazed tiles), set around the lower walls of the nave and chancel.

WAYPOINT LISTS

All waypoints are quoted positions using the WGS84 Datum in Latitude and Longitude format. For notes on using GPS on Madeira, see pages 24. GPS files for these routes are available in GPX Format files as downloads from Discovery Walking Guides Ltd.; for more details see www.walking.demon.co.uk or www.dwgwalking.co.uk

1

Boca da Corrida - Fontes

Wp	North	West
101	32.710974	16.986671
102	32.711850	16.993910
103	32.713490	16.996990
104	32.715380	16.997530
105	32.717090	16.999860
106	32.717410	17.000070
107	32.716140	17.001910
108	32.715920	17.002410
109	32.715050	17.009280
110	32.718600	17.010050
111	32.717102	17.013636
112	32.702090	17.020800

2

Boca da Corrida - Pico Grande

Wp	North	West
201	32.710940	16.986590
202	32.716580	16.989990
203	32.720717	16.990457
204	32.722680	16.989130
205	32.730930	16.985740
206	32.736780	16.987590

3

Boca dos Namorados - Nun's Valley

Wp	North	West
301	32.695430	16.978320
302	32.702360	16.978560
303	32.705410	16.974560
304	32.705820	16.974250
305	32.713960	16.969610
306	32.719880	16.964390

4

Camara de Lobos - Cabo Girao

Wp	North	West
401	32.676010	16.981270
402	32.676100	16.990380
403	32.681180	16.992010
404	32.680610	16.995720
405	32.664580	16.993650
406	32.663260	17.002110
407	32.656980	17.005070
408	32.656470	17.004420

5

Levada do Norte - Cabo Girão

Wp	North	West
501	32.680760	17.040020
502	32.685100	17.041130
503	32.688630	17.032780
504	32.688150	17.031990
505	32.692000	17.038800
506	32.702190	17.031970
507	32.701520	17.030560
508	32.702410	17.027750
509	32.704570	17.029920
510	32.711380	17.028220
511	32.715420	17.026560

6

Levada do Norte - Encumeada

Wp	North	West
601	32.754040	17.019300
602	32.751790	17.026550
603	32.751270	17.028220
604	32.746930	17.032790
605	32.744290	17.039050

7

Monte to Bom Sucesso

Wp	North	West
701	32.676040	16.899480
702	32.678050	16.895960
703	32.679180	16.893970
704	32.677790	16.893380
705	32.676370	16.894980
706	32.675460	16.894850
707	32.673540	16.894960
708	32.671230	16.895170
709	32.669780	16.895180
710	32.669130	16.895380
711	32.666540	16.896970
712	32.665670	16.896130
713	32.662100	16.897330
714	32.658810	16.898720
715	32.657130	16.898880
716	32.656410	16.900410
717	32.648040	16.904540

8

Pico do Areeiro

Wp	North	West
801	32.734957	16.928491
802	32.735820	16.927560
803	32.736360	16.924720
804	32.735470	16.928750
805	32.735690	16.928670
806	32.739220	16.933540

9

Pico das Pedras - Queimadas

Wp	North	West
901	32.779770	16.896810
902	32.779530	16.899530
903	32.781230	16.902710
904	32.780860	16.906820
905	32.783720	16.905830

10

Abrigo do Pastor

Wp	North	West
1001	32.695380	16.877390
1002	32.694854	16.876709
1003	32.695510	16.873050
1004	32.697181	16.875300
1005	32.699430	16.873310
1006	32.698420	16.876420
1007	32.697910	16.880540
1008	32.697883	16.881375
1009	32.696194	16.878654

11

Ribeira Frio - Santo da Serra

Wp	North	West
1101	32.734060	16.886120
1102	32.739220	16.881610
1103	32.736960	16.876650
1104	32.737730	16.872340
1105	32.733990	16.870710
1106	32.732140	16.866930
1107	32.735360	16.865510
1108	32.736010	16.863930
1109	32.735720	16.857540
1110	32.740540	16.857920
1111	32.739000	16.849990
1112	32.739670	16.847690
1113	32.737170	16.847730
1114	32.733087	16.840284

1115	32.727955	16.829150
1116	32.724593	16.819936

12

Santo da Serra - Serrado das Ameixieiras

Wp	North	West
1201	32.724540	16.820050
1202	32.723190	16.821680
1203	32.713270	16.822820
1204	32.712510	16.821120
1205	32.712170	16.819140
1206	32.709810	16.821430
1207	32.708850	16.820980
1208	32.705930	16.820420
1209	32.707120	16.820540
1210	32.711270	16.821880

13

Levada da Serra do Faial

Wp	North	West
1301	32.724530	16.820070
1302	32.723050	16.821670
1303	32.713370	16.822840
1304	32.711750	16.830690
1305	32.712970	16.836240
1306	32.709500	16.843120
1307	32.705100	16.847620
1308	32.703230	16.847550
1309	32.698440	16.841880
1310	32.693180	16.847790
1311	32.695682	16.862039
1312	32.688430	16.852570
1313	32.685810	16.853130
1314	32.681900	16.845630
1315	32.678980	16.844000

14

Camacha to Monte

Wp	North	West
1401	32.680560	16.844160
1402	32.681790	16.846060
1403	32.686070	16.853510
1404	32.682660	16.853980
1405	32.682780	16.855300
1406	32.677780	16.854130
1407	32.675480	16.863450
1408	32.672300	16.869920
1409	32.674570	16.880350
1410	32.672720	16.882720
1411	32.670990	16.886170
1412	32.670270	16.886440
1413	32.671370	16.886990
1414	32.675830	16.891030
1415	32.675310	16.892230
1416	32.676640	16.892960
1417	32.683420	16.894080
1418	32.682940	16.895040
1419	32.677990	16.896000
1420	32.676480	16.899100
1421	32.676620	16.903010

15

Santana - Calhua - Sao George

Wp	North	West
1501	32.822983	16.885451
1502	32.824210	16.884340
1503	32.826460	16.891230
1504	32.825230	16.891200
1505	32.827180	16.894900
1506	32.828760	16.897510
1507	32.829760	16.898000
1508	32.830560	16.898790
1509	32.834570	16.902640
1510	32.828870	16.901800
1511	32.830820	16.901610
1512	32.827240	16.906610

16

Santana - Ilheu da Rocha do Navio

Wp	North	West
1601	32.805910	16.880600
1602	32.813710	16.879080
1603	32.814710	16.876610
1604	32.813100	16.873370
1605	32.813270	16.872430
1606	32.813330	16.871460
1607	32.811890	16.869730

17

Porto da Cruz Circular

Wp	North	West
1701	32.772760	16.827950
1702	32.772230	16.841510
1703	32.770860	16.843750
1704	32.768130	16.843330
1705	32.767440	16.850630
1706	32.765610	16.846540
1707	32.766700	16.844900
1708	32.763590	16.839110
1709	32.755880	16.836920
1710	32.754540	16.830550
1711	32.751860	16.829740
1712	32.750850	16.829610
1713	32.748650	16.828540
1714	32.753780	16.826880
1715	32.756710	16.831850
1716	32.758150	16.830720
1717	32.758680	16.829470
1718	32.770280	16.827170
1719	32.770330	16.828280
1720	32.771440	16.827980

18

Marocos to Ribeira Seca

Wp	North	West
1801	32.735260	16.804130
1802	32.737830	16.799750
1803	32.741740	16.800480
1804	32.738090	16.791310
1805	32.741150	16.790820
1806	32.740120	16.790280
1807	32.735500	16.785030
1808	32.743920	16.784260
1809	32.745800	16.782790
1810	32.742690	16.781510
1811	32.741990	16.778500
1812	32.750000	16.773210
1813	32.746250	16.773350
1814	32.740930	16.774937

19

Sao Lourenco Circular

Wp	North	West
1901	32.744750	16.715850
1902	32.745250	16.715130
1903	32.743520	16.712600
1904	32.742690	16.713330
1905	32.744320	16.713150
1906	32.743240	16.714740
1907	32.743070	16.715720
1908	32.744110	16.716110

20

Levada da Rocha Vermelha

NWp	North	West
2001	32.753520	17.149790
2002	32.755600	17.142750
2003	32.753320	17.145140
2004	32.748450	17.146570
2005	32.746460	17.147170
2006	32.742950	17.149290
2007	32.739580	17.149660
2008	32.746671	17.149756
2009	32.745590	17.152750
2010	32.741800	17.157900
2011	32.742780	17.159990

21

Rabacal Risco and 25 Fontes

Wp	North	West
2101	32.754940	17.133850
2102	32.753470	17.129190
2103	32.761700	17.134360
2104	32.762420	17.131670
2105	32.760550	17.124320
2106	32.762630	17.129500
2107	32.761900	17.125320
2109	32.765700	17.125470
2108	32.766280	17.129990

2110	32.763660	17.131380
2111	32.762960	17.135210
2112	32.762220	17.136200

22

Ribeira Grande Lajeada Circular

Wp	North	West
2201	32.754380	17.133300
2202	32.753410	17.132550
2203	32.753810	17.126320
2204	32.755600	17.130200
2205	32.757870	17.130010
2206	32.758190	17.125390
2207	32.757606	17.120752
2208	32.756960	17.111180
2209	32.758700	17.107470
2210	32.759410	17.107010
2211	32.759410	17.113930
2212	32.758820	17.103900
2213	32.758230	17.105150
2214	32.756210	17.108970
2215	32.756000	17.111550
2216	32.754330	17.117080
2217	32.754230	17.118300
2218	32.752740	17.121030

23

Around Fanal

Wp	North	West
2301	32.809980	17.140660
2302	32.804390	17.131740
2303	32.806310	17.131210
2304	32.808760	17.128330
2305	32.809910	17.130650

24

Chão da Ribeira Plateau

Wp	North	West
2401	32.801160	17.115360
2402	32.800850	17.115790
2403	32.799452	17.115803
2404	32.797190	17.117740
2405	32.798950	17.115280
2406	32.796860	17.113980
2407	32.793950	17.113220
2408	32.792590	17.113110
2409	32.793435	17.113237
2410	32.809160	17.115110
2411	32.811900	17.112010
2412	32.815160	17.109800
2413	32.816000	17.109570
2414	32.819870	17.108880

25

Estanquinhos- Pico Ruivo do Paúl

Wp	North	West
2501	32.764700	17.082090
2502	32.770080	17.082970
2503	32.772830	17.083830
2504	32.771530	17.080040
2505	32.774570	17.078700
2506	32.776980	17.080140
2507	32.776720	17.079790
2508	32.770630	17.075900

26

Levada do Paúl

Wp	North	West
2601	32.739900	17.102530
2602	32.742713	17.101996
2603	32.742930	17.108790
2604	32.744560	17.115880
2605	32.744120	17.120270
2606	32.747720	17.122370
2607	32.748320	17.125330
2608	32.754610	17.133820

27

Cristo Rei - Levada da Bica da Cana

Wp	North	West
2701	32.739760	17.102470
2702	32.736500	17.101000
2703	32.734850	17.097970
2704	32.735450	17.096860
2705	32.735150	17.096060
2706	32.741180	17.091460
2707	32.741190	17.090320

28

Bica da Cana - Pinaculo

Wp	North	West
2801	32.757490	17.059360
2802	32.756320	17.054810
2803	32.756100	17.055260
2804	32.754280	17.054180
2805	32.754680	17.052210
2806	32.752750	17.050980
2807	32.753030	17.046190
2808	32.754840	17.052780
2809	32.760170	17.057480

29

Encumeada - Folhadal - Ginhas

Wp	North	West
2901	32.754560	17.020730
2902	32.754240	17.019310
2903	32.751390	17.028230
2904	32.753582	17.033718
2905	32.751960	17.039890
2906	32.752400	17.040990
2907	32.760140	17.049200
2908	32.761985	17.049443
2909	32.768868	17.052932
2910	32.774000	17.055540
2911	32.773420	17.047910
2912	32.778320	17.048130
2913	32.776540	17.046000
2914	32.779090	17.049260
2915	32.779820	17.048300
2916	32.781740	17.043800

30

Santa to Porto Moniz

Wp	North	West
3001	32.859870	17.190840
3002	32.859900	17.190230
3003	32.860990	17.186590
3004	32.864430	17.179380
3005	32.863510	17.176040
3006	32.863820	17.175250
3007	32.864280	17.175320
3008	32.865420	17.171450
3009	32.866990	17.168280
3010	32.867310	17.167000

31

Ponta do Pargo to Cabo

Wp	North	West
3101	32.813840	17.246140
3102	32.818160	17.244650
3103	32.820130	17.243110
3104	32.821920	17.241300
3105	32.822100	17.240290
3106	32.823840	17.240810
3107	32.825390	17.239970
3108	32.826130	17.238490
3109	32.828310	17.238690
3110	32.829190	17.238290
3111	32.832140	17.234880
3112	32.829830	17.240730

32

Levada Moinho - Porta - Achadas da Cruz

Wp	North	West
3201	32.845780	17.193700
3202	32.842060	17.191870
3203	32.840000	17.193820
3204	32.839970	17.196900
3205	32.840470	17.198680
3206	32.839890	17.204900
3207	32.837720	17.204700
3208	32.840990	17.206310

33

Levada da Ribeira da Janela

Wp	North	West
3301	32.851710	17.166540
3302	32.839560	17.173550
3303	32.836020	17.180200

34

Levada Nova - Ponta do Pargo

Wp	North	West
3401	32.776720	17.220650
3402	32.774910	17.226310
3403	32.777690	17.228240
3404	32.784710	17.231960
3405	32.787393	17.225442
3406	32.787480	17.233360
3407	32.795350	17.233750
3408	32.800810	17.234980
3409	32.806820	17.232760
3410	32.809130	17.239350
3411	32.811243	17.244425

35

Fajã da Ovellha - Paúl do Mar

Wp	North	West
3501	32.776720	17.220650
3502	32.774910	17.226310
3503	32.777690	17.228240
3504	32.774350	17.232900
3505	32.773990	17.234630
3506	32.773390	17.232300
3507	32.772190	17.235930
3508	32.770180	17.236420
3509	32.768170	17.235380
3510	32.765750	17.234960
3511	32.764770	17.234520
3512	32.754960	17.228280
3513	32.753180	17.225160

36

Prazeres - Jardim do Mar

Wp	North	West
3601	32.752500	17.216920
3602	32.752960	17.214240
3603	32.748470	17.210190
3604	32.745040	17.210720
3605	32.740520	17.211160
3606	32.739350	17.210640
3607	32.738920	17.211300
3608	32.735400	17.208750
3609	32.737780	17.211570

37

Levada Nova Prazeres - Calheta

Wp	North	West
3701	32.754120	17.203320
3702	32.756540	17.199960
3703	32.759740	17.184380
3704	32.750400	17.186430
3705	32.747980	17.183570
3706	32.747830	17.175410
3707	32.759020	17.166980
3708	32.742680	17.160000
3709	32.737000	17.166450
3710	32.731710	17.176150
3711	32.730270	17.177990

38

Loreto to Canhas

Wp	North	West
3801	32.726640	17.144500
3802	32.724390	17.139100
3803	32.723990	17.137610
3804	32.721910	17.137120
3805	32.720670	17.137060
3806	32.718820	17.137080
3807	32.722430	17.133100
3808	32.723790	17.130940
3809	32.724800	17.128530
3810	32.726900	17.124660
3811	32.719160	17.127810
3812	32.716613	17.125375
3813	32.712000	17.117150
3814	32.709060	17.116960
3815	32.698298	17.119558

39

Loreto - Madelena do Mar

Wp	North	West
3901	32.726640	17.144500
3902	32.724390	17.139100
3903	32.723990	17.137610
3904	32.721910	17.137120
3905	32.720670	17.137060
3906	32.718820	17.137080
3907	32.722430	17.133100
3908	32.723790	17.130970
3909	32.714550	17.138140
3910	32.711490	17.138090
3911	32.710440	17.138400
3912	32.707640	17.139090
3913	32.707190	17.137980
3914	32.708880	17.137220
3915	32.707490	17.134990
3916	32.706190	17.135190
3917	32.705950	17.135190
3918	32.704350	17.135290
3919	32.703680	17.135110
3920	32.702840	17.135900
3921	32.702925	17.137332

40

Lombada da Ponta do Sol

Wp	North	West
4001	32.689440	17.091650

APPENDIX A USEFUL INFORMATION

Please note that, while the following information is believed to be correct at the time of printing, it is advisable to check on opening hours etc. on arrival. Ask in tourist offices, or your hotel reception staff may be able to help. The dial code for Madeira from overseas is + 351.

TAXIS

Calheta	291 822 423	Maroços & Ribeira Seca	917840983
Estrela da Calheta	966038547 919695861	Monte	
Cabo Girão	965010106	Babosas Square	917242216 291782158
Camacha	291 922185	Ponta Delgada	291 862449
Cãmara de Lobos	291 942700 291 942407	Ponta do Sol	291 972110
Campanario	291 953601	Porto da Cruz	291 562411
Caniçal	291 961989 917323630	Paúl do Mar	963075612
Caniço	291 932156 291 933022	Porto Moniz/Lamaceiros	
Canhas	291 972470 917323630 919514041		291 852243 - 291 852164 - 966045524
Faial	291 572416	Ponta do Pargo	965013090
Fontes & Jardim da Serra	966033815	Amparo	967425752
Funchal:		Cabo	291 882165
Central	291 222000	Ribeira Brava	291 952349 291 952606 966045604
Avenida do Mar	291 523473		
Lido	291 741412	Ribeira da Janela	291 852166 917842059
Mercada	291 226400	Ribeiro Frio	291 782158
Martinho	291 765620	Santa Cruz	291 524888
Nazaré	291 762780	Santana	969716933 291 572540 291 572788
Ginhas	291 846149	Santo da Serra	962928021 291 522100
Gaula	291 526643	São Vicente	291 842238 291 842929
Machico	291 962480 291962220 291963666		

USEFUL PHONE NUMBERS

Emergencies	112	Motorway Assistance(V1)	800 290 290
Airport	291 520 888	Motorway Assistance (VE)	800 203 040
Police	291 208 200	Coastguard	291 700 112

TOURIST INFORMATION

The Tourist Offices listed below are the 'official' Madeira Tourist Authority offices.

Main Tourist Office, Funchal 291 211 900/902
Direcção Regional do Turismo info@madeiratourism.org
Avenida Arriaga No 18, 9004-519 Funchal www.madeiratourism.org
Mon to Fri 9.00 a.m. - 8.00 p.m. Sat & Sun 9.00 a.m. - 6.00 p.m.

Tourist Office, Monumental Lido 291 775254
C.C. Monumental Lido, Estrada Monumental, 284, 9000-100 Funchal
Mon to Fri 9.00 a.m. - 8.00 p.m. Sat 9.00 a.m. - 2.00 p.m.

Tourist Office at Airport, Santa Catarina de Baixo, 9100 Santa Cruz 291 524933
Daily 9.00 a.m. - midnight

Tourist Office, Caniço, 9125 Caniço de Baixo 291 932919
Mon to Fri 9.00 a.m. - 12.30 p.m. & 2.00 p.m. - 5.30 p.m.

Tourist Office, Machico, Forte Nossa Senhora do Amparo, 9200 Machico 291 962289
Mon to Fri 9.00 a.m. - 12.30 p.m. Sat 09.30 a.m. - 12.00 noon

Tourist Office, Ribeira Brava, Forte de São Bento, 9350 Ribeira Brava 291 951675
Mon to Fri 9.00 a.m. - 12.30 p.m. & 2.00 p.m. - 5.00 p.m. Sat 9.30 a.m. - 12.00 noon

Tourist Office, Lugar de Baixo, Centro de Observação de Natureza 291 972850
Lagoa - Lugar de Baixo, 9860,110 Ponta do Sol
Mon to Fri 2.00 p.m.- 5.00 p.m. Sat 9.30 a.m. - 12.00 noon

Tourist Office, Cãmara de Lobos, Town Hall 921 943470
Cãmara de Lobos, Largo de Republica, 9300 Cãmara de Lobos
Mon to Fri 9.00 a.m. - 12.30 p.m. & 2.00 p.m. - 5.00 p.m. Sat 9.30 a.m. - 12.00 noon

Tourist Office, Porto Moniz, 9270 Porto Moniz 291 852594
Mon - Fri 10.00 a.m. - 3.00 p.m. Sat 12.00 p.m. - 3.00 p.m.
Tourist Office, Santana, Sitio do Serrado, 9230 Santana 291 572 992
Mon to Fri 9.00 a.m. - 12.30 p.m. & 2.00 p.m. - 5.30 p.m. Sat 9.30 a.m. - 12.00 noon
Tourist Office, Porto Santo 291 985189
Avenida Henrique Vieira e Castro, Porto Santo 9400
Mon to Fri 9.00 a.m. - 5.30 p.m. Sat 10.00 a.m. - 12.30 p.m.

APPENDIX B
GARDENS, NATURE RESERVES, NATURAL HISTORY MUSEUMS, FESTIVALS & EVENTS

We advise that you check that the opening times listed below are still current by visiting the garden websites (where available) or ask in the Tourist Information Offices.

GARDENS

Monte Palace Tropical Garden (and museum) www.montepalace.com
Caminho do Monte, Monte *Open daily (not Christmas Day) 9.30 a.m. - 6 p.m.*
Monte Municipal Park Monte *Open daily - no admission charge*
Jardim Botânico da Madeira www.sra.pt/jarbot
Quinta do Bom Sucesso, Funchal *Open daily (not Christmas Day) 9.00 a.m. - 6 p.m.*
Quinta das Cruzes (gardens and museum) www.sra.pt/jarbot/
Santa Clara, Funchal *Open Monday to Friday 11.00 a.m. - 17.00 p.m.*
Quinta Vigia, Avenida do Infante www.sra.pt/jarbot
Parque de Santa Catarina, Funchal *Monday to Friday 9.00 a.m. - 5 p.m.*
Municipal Dona Amélia Garden, Avenida Arriaga, Funchal www.sra.pt/jarbot
Municipal Garden Avenida Arriaga, Funchal *Public park - no admission charge*
Parque de Santa Catarina Funchal *Open daily - no admission charge*
Palheiro Gardens www.madeira-gardens.com
Palheiro Ferreiro *Open Monday to Friday 10.00 a.m. - 4.30 p.m.*
Quinta da Boa Vista, Rua do Lombo da Boa Vista
Funchal *Open Monday to Saturday 9.00 a.m. - 5.30 p.m.*
Orchid Garden, Rua Pita da Silva, Funchal www.madeiraorchids.com
Open daily 9.30 a.m. - 6 p.m.
Quinta do Arco Rose Garden, Arco de São Jorge www.quintadoarco.com
Open daily 11.00 a.m. - 6 p.m.
Quinta Magnólia Gardens Rua do Dr Pita, Funchal *Open daily - no admission charge*
Quinta da Serra close the square, Santo da Serra *Open daily - no admission charge*
*See **Walk 12** for details*

NATURE RESERVES

Parque Ecológico do Funchal Tel: 291 784700
See Walk 8 for details. *No admission charge*
Núcleo de Dragoeiros das Neves Tel: 291 795155
. *(No admission charge) Opening Hours: Daily 9.00 a.m. - 6.00 p.m.*
Parque Florestal Ribeiro Frio *(No admission charge) Open daily*
Espaço Natural Floresta Laurissilva *See **Walk 24** for details* Tel: 291 854033
Chão da Ribeira, Seixal, Porto Moniz *(No admission charge) Open daily*
Rocha do Navio Nature Reserve *See **Walk 16** for details*

NATURAL HISTORY MUSEUMS

Museu Municipal do Funchal (Natural History Museum and Aquarium) Tel: 291 229761
In the beautiful **Palácio de São Pedro**. Permanent exhibitions of fauna, flora and geology including fish, bird and mammal specimens, insects, plants, minerals, rocks and fossils.
Opening hours: Tues to Fri 10.00 a.m. - 6.00 p.m. Sat & Sun 12.00 noon - 6.00 p.m.
Aquário da Madeira Porto Moniz www.aquariodamadeira.com
Opening Hours: Daily 9.00 a.m. - 6.00 p.m
.

Volcano Centre and Caves São Vicente

Opening Hours: Daily 9.00 a.m. - 7.00 p.m.

Núcleo Museológico - Rota da Cal (The Lime Route) Tel: 291 842023

Open daily

Museu da Baleia (Whale Museum) Tel: 291 961858

Situated in **Caniçal** in a new purpose-built building, the museum is a testament to the history of Madeiran whaling.

THINGS TO DO Note: this list is not exhaustive.

SAILING/WHALE & DOLPHIN WATCHING & TRIPS TO THE DESERTAS ISLANDS

Gavião, Luxury Yacht 291 241124 / 291 706401
Marina do Funchal, 9000-055 Funchal gaviaomadeira@netmadeira.com
Bonita da Madeira "Dream Cruises" 291 762 218 291 763345
Estrada Monumental 187 info@bonita-da-madeira.com
9000-100 Funchal www.bonita-da-madeira.com

SAILING/WHALE & DOLPHIN WATCHING

Beluga Submarine Vision -Glass Bottom Boat 967 044217
Visões Aquadélicas. Lda belugasubmarine@hotmail.com
Ilhéu Ketch departs from Calheta/Madalena da Mar 291 974044 968 768194
Contact skipper: João Vieira www.ilheu-sailing.com joaovilheu@hotmail.com
Ribeira Brava - Restored Fishing Vessel 963 103 762 291 771 582
Lobosonda, Calheta Marine, Calheta lobosonda@sapo.pt
Santa Maria (Replica of Columbus's vessel) 291 220327
Marina - Funchal, 9000-055 Funchal nau.santa.maria@mail.telepac.pt
Sea Born, Sea Born Kiosk 291 231 312 - 919 916 221
Marina do Funchal seaborn@madeira.com

BIRD WATCHING

Horizonte do Atlántico, Rua do Quebra Costas, 28, 2 291 280024 / 963 390796
9000-034 Funchal www.venturadomar@iol.pt www.venturadomar.com
Madeira Wind Birds, Rua da Pena, 10 G 291 723171
9050-099 Funchal info@madeirabirds.com www.madeirabirds.com

CLIMBING & CANYONING

Horizonte do Atlántico, Rua do Quebra Costas, 28, 2 963 390796 / 291 280024
9000-034 Funchal www.venturadomar.com www.venturadomar@iol.pt
Parque Ecológico do Funchal 291 784 700
Nuno Cunha Canyoning Guide 967766864
Calhua, São Jorge cardosoecunha@gmail.com

FESTIVALS/ANNUAL EVENTS

For the exact dates when each of these annual events will take place, see www.madeiratourism.org

Walking Festival	January
Carnival	mid-February
Flower Festival	3 day event towards end April
Atlantic Festival	June
Wine Festival	end August/beginning September
Festival of the Bands	mid-October
Christmas Lights/New Year Celebrations	December/January

APPENDIX C (1) OFFICIAL RECOMMENDED TRAILS FOR HIKERS

PR01	Vereda do Areeiro	PR08	Vereda da Ponta de São Lourenço
PR01.1	Vereda da Ilha	PR09	Levada do Caldeirão Verde
PR01.2	Vereda do Pico Ruivo -	PR10	Levada do Furado
PR01.3	Vereda do Encumeada -	PR11	Vereda dos Balcões
PR02	Vereda do Urzal - (Not yet officially open as at Spring 2011)	PR12	Caminho Real da Encumeada
		PR13	Vereda do Fanal
PR03	Vereda do Burro	PR14	Levada dos Cedros
PR03.1	Vereda do Monte	PR15	Vereda da Ribeira da Janela
PR04	Vereda do Barreiro	PR16	Levada da Fajã do Rodriques
PR05	Vereda das Funduras	PR17	Caminho do Pináculo e Folhadal
PR06	Levada das 25 Fontes	PR18	Levada do Rei
PR06.1	Levada do Risco	PR19	Caminho Real do Paúl do Mar
PR07	Levada do Moinho	PR20	Vereda do Jardim do Mar

APPENDIX C (2) DISABLED ROUTES

"Tourism and leisure activities have become basic aspects of modern society. The right to enjoy them is a quality of life indicator and an element of social integration, just as the right to education and work.

Leisure enjoyment forms part of a satisfying human experience and is fundamental for the physical, psychological and social development of the individual. In the case of the disabled, moreover, it can be considered a vitally important factor towards complete integration.''

Taken from the Tourmac website www.tourmac.info/discapacided/index the above sets out the philosophy behind this imaginative programme, which has been funded by the European Union and the contracting Governments of Spain and Portugal, who have acquired the (Joelette) cycles, so that the disabled can enjoy hiking in this part of the world.

Joelettes (adapted wheelchairs) are offered free of charge to both local inhabitants and visitors, as a means of ensuring that no member of the family needs to miss out when the rest go walking. These routes are not suitable for normal wheelchair access; use of the adapted cycles requires either previous experience, or the services of the specialized guides.

The programme, managed in Madeira by the Forestry Service in conjunction with the Fire and Ambulance Service (The Bombeiros), currently has two routes designated for the purpose, established and signed with PB JOELLETTE information panels, field code markings and fingerposts. Others will be considered on request, subject to suitable terrain.

PBTTJOELETTE - From **Portela** to **Fajã dos Rolos** (close to **Machico**)
Distance 12.6 km - Descent 165 m.
Follows and intersects with Walk 15 in Walk! Madeira (PR5 - Vereda das Funduras).
PR JOEL - **Queimadas** (**Santana**) to **Pico das Pedras**
Distance 2.1 km - Descent/Ascent 20 m. For directions see Walk 9 in this publication.

ROUTE FOR THE BLIND
PR JOEL - **Queimadas** (**Santana**) to **Pico das Pedras**
Distance 2.1 km - Descent/Ascent 20 m. For directions see Walk 9 in this publication.

Contacts: -
Direcção Regional das Florestas/Secretaria Regional Ambiente Recourses Naturais
Sra. Eng. Ana Sé Tel: 291 740060Fax: 291 74065
Associação dos Bombeiros Voluntários da Calheta Sr. João Alegria - Comandante
Corporação dos Bombeiros da Calheta Tel: 291 827204 Fax: 291 827392 Mob: 96 4785443
Associação dos Bombeiros Voluntários da Santana
Sr. Nuno - Adjunto do Comandante da Corporação dos Bombeiros Santana
Sr. José Antonio Freitas - Comandante Tel: 291 570110 Fax:291570119 Mob 964786895

Casado Povo de Machico
Sr Emanuel Spinola - Presidente da Casa do Povo de Machico
Tel: 291 966098 Fax: 291 966384 Mob: 913 458384

CYCLING ROUTES

PBTTJOELETTE - From **Portela** to **Fajã dos Rolos** (eastern route close to **Machico**) Distance 12.6 km - Descent 165 m. Follows and intersects with our Walk 15 (PR5 - Verada das Funduras)
PBTT1 - From **Cruzinhas**, **Fonte do Bispo** to **São Lourenço**, **Fajá da Ovelha** (western route starting close to the Forestry Post at **Fonte do Bispo**; off the ER210). Descent c.700m
PBTT2 - **Lombada dos Cedros** (northern route starting from **Fonte do Bispo**) - Details not available at time of printing.

APPENDIX D BIBLIOGRAPHY

MAPS

Madeira Tour & Trail Super-Durable Map (pub. Discovery Walking Guides Ltd.). Regularly re-researched and updated, highly detailed and accurate. For the latest version see www.walking.demon.co.uk or www.amazon.co.uk
Madeira Bus & Touring Map (pub. Discovery Walking Guides Ltd.). For the latest edition see websites as above.

WALKING GUIDES

Walk! Madeira with Shirley & Mike Whitehead (3rd edition) (ISBN 9781904946694 pub. 2010 Discovery Walking Guides Ltd).
Companion to *Shirley Whitehead's Madeira Walks*. 40 walks from gentle strolls to mountain challenges, detailed maps and GPS data for each route, information on flora, fauna and places of interest.

REFERENCE BOOKS

Flora Endémica da Madeira (Roberto Jardim/David Fransisco pub.2000 ISBN 9728622007)
Madeira Plants and Flowers (L O Franquinho/A Da Costa pub.1999 ISBN 972917721X)
Madeira's Natural History in a Nutshell (Peter Sziemer pub.2000 ISBN 9729177317)
Madeira - A Botanical Melting Pot (Dr Susanne Lipps pub.2006 ISBN 3938282096)
SPEA - Where to Watch Birds in the Madeira Archipelago (Cláudia Delgado pub.2006 ISBN 9729901899)
Prion Birdwatchers' Guide to Portugal and Madeira (H Costa, C C Moore, G Elias (pub. Prion Birdwatchers' Guide)
Field Guide to the Birds of the Atlantic Islands: Canary Islands, Madeira, Azores, Cape Verde (Tony Clarke, Chris Orgill (Illustrator), Tony Disley pub.2006 Christopher Helm Publishers Ltd ISBN 0713660236)
A Field Guide to the Butterflies of the Ecological Park and Madeiran Archipelago (Andrew Wakeham-Dawson, Michael Salmon, António Franquinho Aguiar - published by the Cãmara Municipal do Funchal

PUBLICATIONS FOR BIRD WATCHING ENTHUSIASTS

SPEA-Madeira *Discover the Birds of Laurissilva IBA (and surrounding areas)*
Discover the Birds of Ponta do Pargo IBA
- available from SPEA-Madeira (Portuguese Society for the Protection of Birds, Travessa das Torres, Old Town, 9060-314 Funchal Tel: 291 241 210 www.spea.pt madeira@spea.pt
Discover the Birds of Funchal Ecological Park Parque Ecológico do Funchal Madeira

LOCAL NEWSPAPERS AND MAGAZINES IN ENGLISH

THE BRIT
The only English language newspaper currently available. Monthly, free from hotels, 1.50 euros from newsagents. Shirley contributes the regular series: 'Walking in Madeira with Shirley Whitehead'.
ESSENTIAL MADEIRA ISLANDS
A glossy leisure and lifestyle magazine produced bi-monthly by a Portuguese company, focusing on Art, Design, Fashion, Nature and Golf, as well as Eating Out. 3.50 euros a copy.

APPENDIX E BUS INFORMATION

Madeira's remarkable network of bus services is cheap, usually punctual and is a fun way to see the island and to access some walking routes. However, finding out which bus you need can be confusing as several operators run the services, sometimes using the same bus numbers for entirely different routes. Timetable changes happen quite frequently, so use this information as a guide; pick up the latest details in Madeira's tourist offices and information/ticket kiosks along the main **Avenida do Mar**; most of the main bus stops are spread along the *avenida* or in the adjoining streets.

The main bus operator for the **Funchal** region is Horários do Funchal, offering about fifty routes. They have a special cheap seven-day ticket for a week's travel. Operators of out of town and country routes include SAM, Rodoeste, and EACL.

To get the very best out of Madeira's bus services, arm yourself with the *Madeira Bus & Touring Map* (pub. Discovery Walking Guides Ltd) which includes details of all the routes, itineraries, timetables and more, and visit www.horariosdofunchal.pt www.rodoeste.pt www.sam.pt

ORANGE town bus route numbers/destinations:

1	Ponta da Laranjeira	23	Livramento
2	Papagaio Verde	24	Pizo (industrial zone)
3	Lombada	25	Levada de Santa Luzia (via Til)
4	Pico dos Barcelos	26	Levada de Santa Luzia (via Pena)
5	Lido	27	Caminho de Ferro
7	Travessa do Pomar	28	Dr. João
8	Santa Quiteria (via Barreiros)	29	Curral dos Romeiros
8A	Santa Quiteria	30	Largo do Miranda
9	Courelas	31	Jardim Botânico
10	Chamorra	32	Rochinha
11	Trapiche	33	Balancal
12	Jamboto (via Hospital)	34	Canto do Muro
13	Jamboto (via Viveiros)	34A	Caminho do Pasto
14	Álamos	35	Praia Formosa
15	Santana	37	Palheiro Ferreiro
15A	Achada	38	Cancela
16	Santa Quitéria	39	Montanha
16A	Pinheiro das Voltas	40	Quinta da Rocha
17	Lombo Segundo	42	Alegria
18	São João	43	Romeiras
19	Levada da Corujeira (via Pena)	44	Nazaré(via Virtudes)
19	Levada da Corujeira (via Til)	45	Nazaré (via Barreiros)
20	Monte (via Corujeira de Dentro)	46	Ribeira Grande
21	Monte (via Largo da Fonte)	47	São João Latrão
22	Babosas		

Country buses by company/colour

From/To **Funchal**

HORÁRIOS	YELLOW	SAM	CREAM/GREEN
RODOESTE	CREAM/RED	EACL	CREAM/RED

Route numbers/destinations (from Funchal)

2	Assomada	29	Camacha	110	Noguiera
3	Estreito de Cãmara de Lobos	53	Faial	113	Machico, Caniçal
		60	Boqueirão	114	Noguiera
4	Madalena do Mar	77	Santo da Serra	115	Estreito da Calheta
6	Boaventura	78	Machico, Faial	123	Campanário
7	Ribeira Brava	81	Curral das Freiras	138	São Jorge
20	Santo da Serra	96	Corticeiras	139	Porto Moniz
23	Machico	103	Arco de São Jorge	142	Ponta do Pargo
25	Santo da Serra	107	Ponta do Pargo	148	Boa Morte

GLOSSARY

In addition to Portuguese words used in the text, we include other frequently encountered local words.

A

achada plateau
aeroporto airport
água water
alto high
aquário aquarium
autocarro bus
azulejos blue & white glazed tiles

B

baía bay
baixo low
bica spring
boca mountain pass

C

caldeirão cauldron shaped crater/rock basin
caminho path, country road
campo field, plain
caniço reed
casa de cha tea house, café
centro civico civic centre
centro de saudé medical centre
choupana hut, cottage
cima above
colmos traditional triangular house
correios post office
cova cavern
cruz cross
curral animal pen

E

estrada road
expresso motorway

F

faial beech trees
fajã region, parish
fio cable lift
fonte spring
furado levada tunnel

G

gaviota gull

I

ilhéu island

J

jardim garden

L

lago/lagoa lake, pool
lamaceiros marsh land
levada water channel
lombada mountain ridge

M

mar sea
mercado market
miradouro viewing point
moinho mill
monte mountain

P

palheiro thatched cottage/animal shelter
palmeira palm
paragem bus stop
pastelaria cake shop
paúl marshland
pedagógica school, college
penha cliff, ridge
pico peak (mountain)
poço well
poio agricultural terrace
pomar orchard
ponte bridge
porto port
posto florestal forest house
pousada government run hotel

Q

quebrada steep slope, ravine
quinta farm house, country manor

R

ribeira river
risco danger

S

serra mountain range
sol sun

T

teleférico cable car
torre tower

V

vale valley

PLACE NAMES INDEX

The following index includes place names in Portuguese and some of the most commonly used English equivalents.